Round the World Flying

The journal of a Scottish emigrant's voyage from London
to Melbourne on the clipper *Macduff* in 1869

EDITED BY CAROL McNEILL

© Carol McNeill
2008

First published 2008

With assistance from Fife Council Arts and Heritage Grant.

ISBN 978-0-9534686-2-1

Published by
Fife Publicity
fifepublicity@ukonline.co.uk
www.carolmcneill.co.uk

Printed by
Multiprint, Kirkcaldy
Telephone 01592 240755
www.multiprint.tv

Cover design, Jim Swan
Front cover: Clipper *Macduff* entering Port Phillip Heads, 1st December 1865
Painting by George Frederick Gregory (1815-1887) (National Library of Australia)
Back cover: Island of Gigha (Kenneth Allan); Sailing ships in Port Melbourne (State Library of Victoria)

Dedicated to the memory of Alick Macneill who left his native island of Gigha to seek a new life in Australia in 1869

Introduction

When Alexander Macneill emigrated from Scotland to Australia in 1869 on board the clipper *Macduff*, he kept a diary recording his 75 days at sea. His purpose was to send it to his family back home, and this he did; but he probably never imagined that his words – beautifully written in the copperplate script of the day on flimsy paper – would survive around 140 years to give a vivid first-hand account of his voyage to what must have been an unknown country and conditions.

Alick (as his family called him) was born on 14 May 1848 on the small island of Gigha off the west coast of Kintyre, on the west of Scotland. The 1851 census shows that his family lived in Achnaha Ferry House where his father Archibald was the ferryman between Gigha and Tayinloan on the Kintyre mainland. Archibald and his wife Margaret had seven children – Archibald (born 1840), John (1844), Malcolm (1846), Alick, Donald (1850), Margaret (1852) and Catherine who was born in 1855.

Achnaha was a small croft, mentioned in the Gigha Kirk Session records as early as 1799 when the ferryman Donald McQuilken was rebuked for collecting oats and transporting them to Kilberry on a Sunday. Archibald Macneill took over the job in 1851, when the ferry was an open wooden boat with heavy oars, and kept it until his death in 1885. There are no records available regarding his duties, but it's likely that they were very similar to those of the next man to take up the post, John Wotherspoon, who had his terms and conditions set out clearly by the then owner of the island, W. J. Scarlett. Wotherspoon lived in Ferry Croft "except for that piece surrounding the house of Mrs Macneill [Archibald's widow] which she rents" and was allowed to keep all the ferry dues. These were specific: "One passenger two shillings, and where more than one passenger, sixpence each; one horse four shillings; every additional horse two shillings; one cow two shillings; every additional cow one shilling; sheep per head threepence; one pig two shillings; if more than four pigs each four pence; bulls and stallions double fare; 2 one-year old stirks to be considered equal to one cow; barley sixpence per quarter; telegram two shillings." In return, the ferryman had to give a free passage to the owner as well as to his family, friends, servants and tradesmen. He was expected to do some work on the estate as well as have time to work on his own croft, and if he went further afield than Tayinloan he had to provide a relief ferryman at his own expense.

The croft house where the Macneills lived is still standing, and it (along with what would have been the byre and hayloft) has since been renovated and restored as a holiday cottage.

Alick went to school on the island (the 1861 Census describes him still on Gigha, age 12, as a student), and the standard of his faultless grammar, spelling and wide vocabulary (prolixity, terra aqueous and animalculae are just some of the words he uses in his diary) is surely a glowing testimony to the high standard of education in a small rural school in the mid-19th century. It's worth remembering that, in common with the rest of the inhabitants of Gigha, his first language would have been Gaelic. Quite probably he would have started learning English only when he began his schooling, and indeed this may help to explain the literary style of his written journal. His descriptions of the ship are often poetic, and today's readers can well imagine the clipper's huge billowing sails making use of every scrap of canvas to catch the available wind. On the seventh day out, he refers to his voyage as "going round the world flying". A week later he says: "It really is a very fine sight to stand at the stern and look upwards at our vast wings which are something like a large hill covered with snow." Further into the voyage, his appreciation of the ship has not diminished: "The cloud of canvas we carry is something enormous, and I should like to see our ship as she now is with all her wings spread, a mile off."

He left Gigha when he was 15 to live in Glasgow "to enter the business of our commercial world," as he puts it. He probably stayed in the west side of the city as he recalls going for a walk with his brother Johnnie on May Day when they bought "two pence worth of milk from the dairy woman in or near Partick". He also refers to some of his family attending Sandyford Church (now Sandyford Henderson Memorial Church) in Kelvinhaugh Street, also in the west of Glasgow. Six years later, he set sail in the *Macduff*, where the passenger list describes him as a clerk, and crossed the equator on his 21st birthday, which he notes is "a curious coincidence and very few I am sure have the same to say".

Initially leaving the peaceful island of Gigha, known as "God's island" with the quiet pace of the life of a small community, to go to the smoke and noise of Glasgow (then called the "second city of the Empire") would have been daunting enough for many a young man. But emigrating (an experience shared by thousands upon thousands of his fellow-Scots who left for Australia, New Zealand, America or Canada in search of a better life) was a huge step into the unknown at that time. There was already a tradition in Kintyre of emigration from necessity: in what became known as the "six wet years" from 1839 when the potato and oat crops failed in the constant rainfall, people began to despair as their staple diet dwindled to starvation level. In 1840, more than 400 people from his neighbouring parish of Killean and Kilkenzie set sail for the other side of the world, a voyage which at that time took four months by sea from Oban.

Perhaps it was the very rawness and potential of Australia which drew these emigrants from Scotland. It was only 34 years before Alick's voyage that a syndicate led by John Batman explored Port Phillip Bay, looking for suitable sites for a settlement in a large area in what is now the northern suburbs of Melbourne. The discovery of gold in Victoria, between around 1851 and the late 1860s, brought with it a huge growth of population and prosperity. (Shortly before Alick left Scotland, two diggers in Victoria came across a nugget of gold weighing more than 210 lbs, the largest mass of gold on record.) By 1869, Melbourne was growing rapidly, with gas lighting, piped water and good sanitation, and spreading into well-defined suburbs with some grand buildings in the more prosperous areas, and by 1881 the census recorded the population of Greater Melbourne at around 300,000.

Newspapers carried advertisements as early as the 1830s encouraging adventurous Britons to emigrate to Australia. One, in August 1832, advertised the "entirely new British-built Coppered and Armed Ship *Westmoreland* leaving London direct to Sydney with leave to land passengers at Hobart Town, Van Dieman's Land". Attention was drawn to two improved selling points for would-be travellers: "Many highly-respectable persons, who cannot afford the expense of a Cabin Passage, having complained of the hardship of being necessitated to associate indiscriminately with Steerage Passengers of every description during so long a voyage, it is intended to have a first and second Steerage Mess in this vessel, by which arrangement this Inconvenience will be obviated; and as passengers from the country have almost invariably been subject to the heavy expense of living in London for several weeks, owing to Vessels being delayed after the time fixed for sailing, this can be effectually avoided, by securing a Passage by this Ship before leaving home, as a positive day of sailing will be fixed, and notice of the same given to the agents."

Another notice in May 1859, placed in the *Aberdeen Journal* by the Government Emigration Agent in the city, set out the terms of assisted passages. "The Colonial Land and Emigration Commissioners are prepared to grant passages to eligible parties on the following terms:

New South Wales and Van Diemen's Land: Agricultural Labourers and the class of Country Labourers generally, children under 14, per head, 10s.

South Australia: 1. Married Agricultural Labourers and their Wives, and Women of the working class, per head, under 45, £1.

2. Married Journeyman Mechanics and Artizans and their Wives per head, under 45, £2.

3. Single Men taken only on same terms as for Victoria.

4. Children under 14, per head, 10s.

Families in which there are more than two children under seven, or more than three under ten years of age, or (for Victoria and South Australia) in which the sons outnumber the daughters, cannot be accepted.

Single Women over thirty-five years of age are ineligible for any of the Colonies."

The inference that single men were definitely not welcome in Australia at that time seems surprising: were they perhaps seen by the authorities not for their skills and muscle-power, but for their presumed tendencies towards drink and womanising? As for these Victorian ladies over 35, they were obviously regarded as being long past their sell-by date.

Rather ironically perhaps, there are many more records available for those emigrants who went out under Australian government schemes than those who paid their own way. Those who applied for government-assisted passages had to give a wide range of information about their age, family status, occupation, religion and literacy, and many of these registers still remain to help their descendants investigate their family trees.

It seems very unlikely that Alick came under the category of assisted passages. It has been impossible so far to discover where he worked and exactly what his job was in Glasgow, or where he worked in Melbourne; but it is probable that he had at least prospects of work in Australia, armed with a good reference from his Scottish employers. It can be assumed that he must have had at least some money behind him when he booked his passage: he travelled cabin class, not steerage, which afforded as much comfort as possible on board ship. His cabin, which he shared with his friend Mr Sanderson from Edinburgh, was "half as large as an ordinary bedroom, with two sleeping berths. The port hole is right above my knees in bed. On the floor is a new carpet and at the door a crimson mat, the latter uncommon and quite a novelty on board. On either sides are our trunks, in the corner the wash stand and above is a long shelf for books etc. All round we have fixed brass knobs for our coats and hats". Cabin class also entitled him to find his boots polished and placed outside his door each morning, and each evening "the bell rang for us to dress for dinner". As well as being able to travel cabin class, he was generous to his shipboard companions: on his birthday he says that "the captain, my berth companion and a few more were treated to wine at my expense," and on the evening before making landfall he notes that "Mr McKellar and I ordered three bottles of champagne to treat the ladies".

The journal itself is an unbound manuscript, rather like a school jotter with no covers, on very thin paper. The transcription has been as faithful to the original as possible, keeping to the punctuation, underlining for emphasis, vocabulary of the day in words such as signalising and diarising, and the habit of putting the first letter of many nouns in upper case. Some errors may have been made in transcribing, due to the faded writing and (particularly in the first and last pages) damage to the manuscript through age. Alick mentions that "I may remark that sometimes I write the original jottings of my diary lying on the first crosstrees of our mizzen mast. It is a favourite place of mine and forms a nice table to lie down on". As well as demonstrating what a competent sailor he was, this points to the fact that he made a fair copy of his notes perhaps at the end of each day, which would account for the uniform neatness of the entries in the journal. He must have sent his diary back from Melbourne at some point, possibly to his brother or sister, as it came to light rolled up and all but forgotten in a family desk in Glasgow.

According to Lloyd's records: "The *Macduff* was a wooden vessel of ship rig, of 1135 tons, built at Aberdeen in 1859 by Alexander Hall and Co. Her principal dimensions were length 219.5 ft, beam 35 ft, and draught 22.1 ft. The *Macduff* was originally owned by a Mr Cruickshank, and registered at Banff. In 1886-87 the *Macduff* was sold to Christian Anker, of Fredrikshald, Norway, at which port she was registered. Although then flying the Norwegian flag the vessel retained the name *Macduff* and it was under this name that she was wrecked about May 16, 1900, when she went ashore near Cape Tormentine, New Brunswick, and filled with water. She was on a voyage from Belfast to Baie Verte, Newfoundland, at the time. When the *Macduff* was engaged in the wool trade in 1874-5 she made the voyage from Melbourne to London in 88 days, and in 1876-77 made the passage from Geelong to London in 82 days."

A contemporary mariner, Captain H.R. Watson, reminiscing about the carvings he saw as a boy in the 1880s around Melbourne piers, wrote: "The figurehead of the *Macduff* will always be engraved on my memory. Be-whiskered, fierce and defiant, grasping his claymore this rugged Scottish chieftain was so lifelike that it almost frightened me."

The middle to the end of the nineteenth century was the golden age of the clippers, those beautiful sailing ships built for speed and elegance with their hundreds of square yards of sail and distinctive slender sharp bows. The first clippers were built in America in the 1840s, and their name comes either from their ability to clip off the time of a voyage or from the phrase 'going at a good clip'. Either way, their speed was legendary, particularly in the famous races between China and Britain with the aim of delivering the first of each season's tea crop which commanded high prices in London.

Ardminish, the only village on the island of Gigha, with the coastline of Kintyre in the distance. The name Gigha is probably Norse in origin and a popular translation is 'God's island', although another meaning could be 'cleft island.' (Kenneth Allan)

This image of the Gigha ferry, which operated from the north end of the island, dates to the 1930s. It shows ferryman George Allan and (on the shore) postmaster Archibald Wilkieson about to go out to meet the steamer to get the mail along with any intrepid passengers or supplies for the island. (Kenneth Allan)

Achnaha ferry croft in Gigha, home of the Macneill family, pictured in the 1930s with the byre and hay shed to the left of the house and showing its proximity to the water's edge. (Kenneth Allan)

Achnaha ferry croft with its adjacent byre pictured in the 1960s. The buildings have now been restored as holiday cottages. (Kenneth Allan)

An earlier north end ferry with its lug sail is pictured in the period of the First World War. It would have been not all that different from the ferry from Gigha to Tayinloan on the mainland of Kintyre which Archibald Macneill, Alick's father, operated from 1851 until his death in 1885. (Kenneth Allan)

A small sailing ship, possibly a schooner, lies at anchor in Ardminish Bay in the 1930s. (Kenneth Allan)

Part of Ardminish village in the 1930s looking up from Rudha Cinn Mhoir showing (from left) the church, Ceol na Mara, the Cottage, shop, post office and house, school house, school, ferry house (formerly the school house) and on the right, Achnaha ferry house and byre with the manse behind. (Kenneth Allan)

A steamer is pictured leaving the south pier on Gigha around 1920. The half-sunk boat in the foreground by the New Quay is a lifeboat from the *Aska* shipwrecked on Cara during the First World War. (Kenneth Allan)

Campbeltown loch, Kintyre, showing a schooner from the Baltic along with other sailing ships around 1900. (MacGrory Collection, Argyll and Bute Library Service)

Sailing ships at the Old Quay in Campbeltown around 1900, with the weigh-house in the foreground. (MacGrory Collection, Argyll and Bute Library Service)

Partick (mentioned in the journal) on the west side of Glasgow, with horse drawn transport and Kelvingrove Art Gallery in the background, pictured around 1900.

Glasgow in the early 1900s was a busy and crowded city which must have seemed a world away from the peace of Gigha.

The clipper *Macduff* in dock. A wooden vessel of ship rig, she was built in 1859 by Alexander Hall and Co. of Aberdeen. 1135 tons, length 219.5 ft, beam 35 ft, and draught 22.1 ft, she was originally registered in Banff. She made 22 voyages from London to Melbourne between 1865 and 1886. Her figurehead of a clansman with a claymore can just be made out in the photograph. She was wrecked in 1900 when she went ashore near Cape Tormentine, New Brunswick.
(State Library of Victoria)

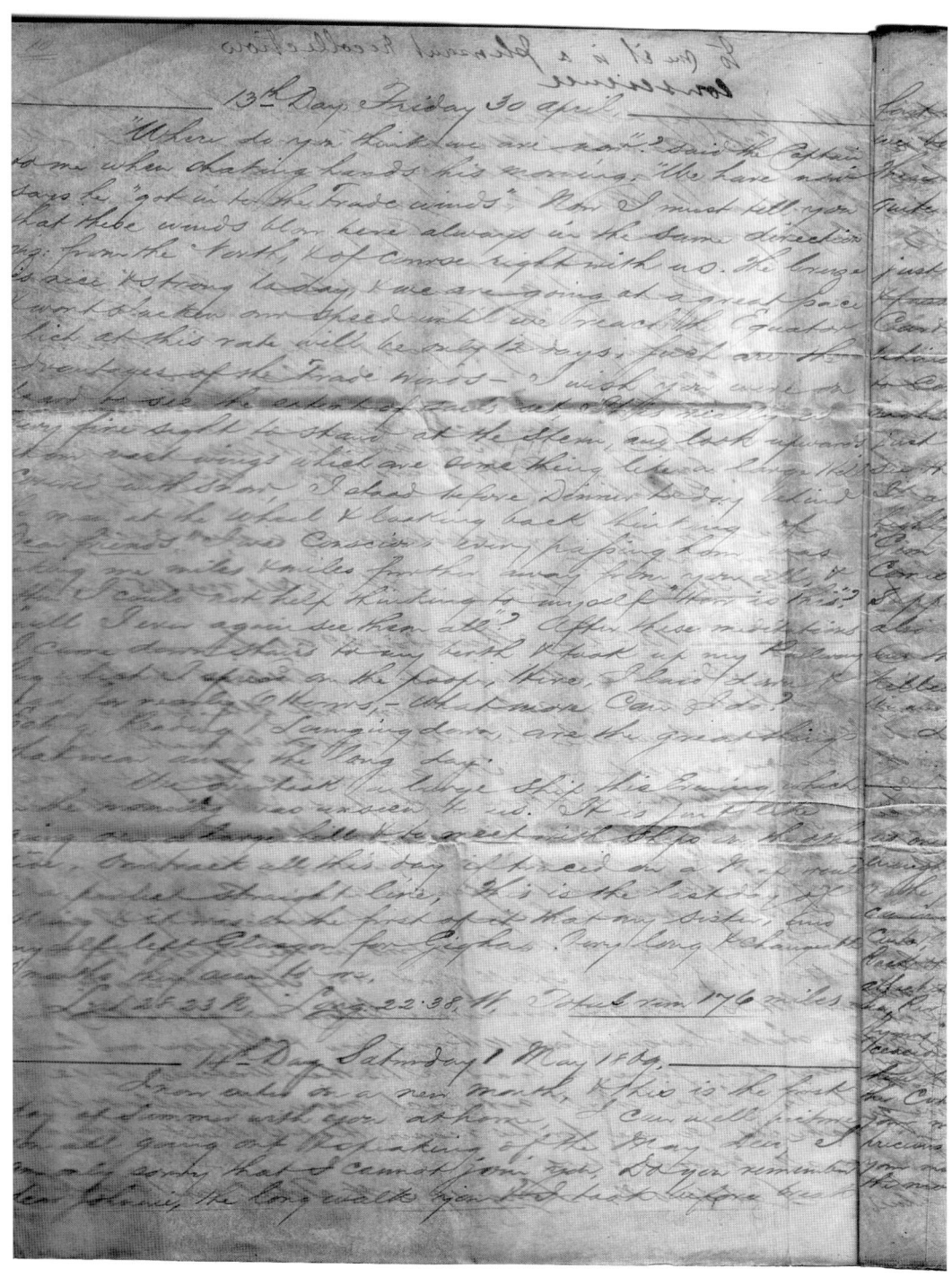

A page of Alick's journal written on board the *Macduff*, transcribed on page 25.

Scottish shipyards quickly followed on by designing their own thoroughbred clippers. The best known are probably *Cutty Sark*, built in Dumbarton by Scott and Linton in 1869 and preserved today at Greenwich, and her greatest rival *Thermopylae*, built in the previous year by Walter Hood and Co. of Aberdeen. Their most memorable China tea trade race was in 1872 when they were neck and neck for part of the journey until *Thermopylae* arrived in British waters a few days ahead of her rival. Other legendary clippers (both built by Robert Steele of Greenock) were *Ariel* and *Taeping* which took part in the closest tea race ever in 1866, with only about a mile separating them at the finish after their 15,000 mile passage from China.

Many of the world's clippers had short lives, often coming to grief in treacherous seas, or with their vulnerability to catching fire with their wooden construction (some all wood and some with iron frames with wooden planking and decks). They finally gave way to the advance of the steamships, more economically viable for both cargo and passengers, and the opening of the Suez Canal.

Although Alick's narrative refers mainly to the passengers, the *Macduff* also carried cargo, and the manifest published in full detail in the Melbourne *Argus* shows the huge and varied amount of goods carried. These included materials for building and industry such as 25,000 slates, reaping machine materials, 276 kegs of nails, 12 barrow wheels, 14 cases of galvanised iron, 20 rolls of lead, 100 boxes of sheet glass, 69 casks of scythe stones, six pieces of printing machines, and eight cases of galvanised iron. There were also 112 packages of furniture, one case of hair seating, 30 cases of chairs, three crates of pictures, two boxes of books for the public library, and a piano. The hold also carried thousands of candles, kippered herrings, crushed sugar, pearl barley, split peas, salad oil, currants and raisins, not to mention Epsom salts and ten cases of castor oil. Cigars, confections, 70 quarter-casks of rum, casks of wine, beer, and 99 cases of brandy were also stowed away safely. On the last night before disembarking, Alick says: "Our anchor has just been slipped but it is too late to get ashore any more tonight. Already there are ever so many Custom House officers on board examining and sealing up our hatches." The more profitable part of clipper voyages came on the homeward journey when they took back Australian wool to service the growing British textile market, and often gold bullion which was entrusted to the fastest clippers for speed and security. In January 1869, the *Times* reported in its shipping news: "The *Macduff*, 76 days from Melbourne arrived Plymouth on Friday. She left Port Phillip Heads October 30th with 11,884 oz. of gold, 4,634 bales of wool, 2,802 hides, 119 packages merchandise, 59 tubs and 53 kegs butter etc. The *Macduff* has beaten the *Star of Peace*, *True Briton*, and *Oriental*."

Records held in the State Library of Victoria state that the *Macduff* made 22 voyages from London to Melbourne between 14 December 1865 and 11 February 1886, once every year except for 1866, and twice in 1867. All the voyages (apart from December 1865 where the Master was Captain Bruce, and October 1878 under Captain Strawbridge) were under the command of Captain Thomas T. Watson, who features prominently in Alick's narrative.

Thomas Watson was obviously a very experienced sea captain who excelled not only in the vital navigation and seamanship, but also kept his finger on the pulse of whatever was happening on board his ship. "I may state that our Captain is a great astronomer and knows all the stars as well as his ship – when they come in sight and when they will be seen last. He can take the time and Lat. from one solitary star." Although he ate with the passengers, and sometimes played deck quoits with them and joined in their entertainment, Captain Watson also made sure his charges behaved themselves. On only the fifth day out, he discovered that one of the young men had tacked a piece of paper up high between two ropes for pistol target practice, and "desperately attacked" the would-be marksman who was in danger of putting the whole mast overboard. When there was a dispute about which of the ladies should lay claim to a bird which had been caught (the feathers of which were in great demand for muffs), he unhooked the bird and set it free.

The captain must surely have found a kindred spirit in Alick, who – brought up on an island with a ferryman father – was thoroughly at home with ships and familiar with nautical terms, while always being keen to find out more. Nearing the end of the voyage, he writes: "I know now every sail and most of the ropes on board," and "the captain showed me the sun through the sextant at 12 when right over our heads... this is the way the Long. and Lat. are taken every day." It was the captain who pointed out the Southern Cross, explained the advantages of changing course to take advantage of catching the Trade Winds, and who was "scarcely in bed at all" when the winds were blowing very hard through the night.

Tracing their voyage on an atlas brings home how vast they must have found the ocean and how vulnerable their craft may have seemed. Once they had left the English coast behind, the only land they saw was the island of Madeira, the Cape Verde islands, and Tristan da Cunha. Seeing other ships was not only a welcome break in the often monotonous days at sea, but was a valuable means of keeping in touch with the folk back home. By "signalising" their ship's name and position, the passengers could be sure that the homeward bound ships would report their details to Lloyd's in London, where they could be picked up by anxious relatives. On other occasions they were able to "speak" to passing ships, using a long-stemmed speaking trumpet for communication.

Being entirely dependent on sail power, the weather was of course all important and strong winds were welcomed. On their fifth day out when a steamship is spotted, he remarks: "We all envy these steamers in this calm weather." It took a month at sea before he is able to report: "A strong breeze has been blowing all day with a good sea. We have not had till now anything worth calling a right breeze. The *Macduff* has proved now what she can do… she is going at a fearful pace with as much wind as she can wish for. At home you would call today a half gale of wind, but on board here it is treated as the best weather possible and our good ship has still full canvas set." By the time their course brought them into the longitude of the Cape of Good Hope, the wind was in their favour. "We have a speed of 12 knots as an average. I am never happier than when we have a gale of wind, then it is a fine sight to see the gallant *Macduff*'s white foam which she sends forth 100 yards before her bows and all round. It would be madness in any steamer to come along side of us for speed. In a right gale we go 16 knots an hour which is equal to 19 miles."

By the time the end of the voyage was in sight, the *Macduff* was making 14 knots and travelling around 300 miles a day in a westerly gale. "She did go then 'just like an evil spirit', as Captain Watson termed it – you must see before you can conceive the power of a ship in the ocean." It was no wonder that these ships carried sail makers on board, as being able to carry out repairs to the sails en route was vital. "All last night it blew very strong; three of our headsails were carried away into ribbons."

The squalls had the almost inevitable result of a man lost overboard. "I regret exceedingly having to relate that one of the steerage passengers was washed overboard at 12 o'clock. A sailor having seen him ran down to the stern and threw a life buoy at him but all in vain. Three sailors jumped into the dinghy, helm was put hard down by the captain's orders. The wind being right after us and the sea running nearly mast high, our ship was in danger of being swamped – seeing this and that it was utterly impossible for a small boat to master such waves, our captain deemed it advisable not to risk the lives of men in such weather as they would be engulfed in an instant. This will cast a gloom all over the ship."

The bad weather also provided some lighter moments: on the third day out, just before the Bay of Biscay, the head steward was "by the pitching of the ship, thrown through the door into Mrs Grant's cabin" – which must have caused the parson's wife some degree of alarm. At meal times, it was difficult to keep the food on the table. "Dr Mason carved the ham and it being a huge size, it commenced to roll. I had my eye on it and having my knife and fork in hand I stuck both in it and saved my clothes. This was the cause of great laughter all round." On another occasion: "At tea it was with great difficulty you could get the cup conveyed to your mouth – some made a nice mess of themselves and others. The doctor was unfortunate enough to get the contents of his neighbour's cup spilled on his knees."

There were various ways to help pass the long days at sea: eating was one of the favourites. Rather as with today's cruise liners, the food was varied and plentiful, with five meals a day served in the saloon, including five-course dinners. He describes this in his very first day at sea: "We had for dinner the following dishes, viz: First choice of all soups, roast beef, roast mutton, pork, Australian beef and fowls, third rice, sago, black cherry and many other puddings and pastry, fourth bread and cheese, fifth fruit consisting of apples, oranges, figs, raisins, almonds, nuts, by which you will perceive we are not meant to starve."

Much of the variety of the menu was due to "30 sheep, 20 pigs and 200 fowl" put on board at the London docks and, in the days before refrigeration, despatched as needed on the voyage; as well as "preserved" milk, beef, fish, eggs. Fruit such as damsons and gooseberries for their daily puddings was also carried, and if only one passenger wanted jam or jelly at teatime, this would be on the table. A butcher, baker, several cooks and four stewards looked after the catering side. There was a "plentiful supply of fresh water on board" but nevertheless, the captain saw to it that as much rainwater was collected in buckets and dishes to augment their supply. The passengers were allocated a gallon of water a day – "which comes to our cabin door with our boots brushed at 7 o'clock every morning" – but the sailors were rationed more strictly and "only allowed a certain quantity of water".

There were the usual shipboard activities – playing quoits on deck and cards in the saloon – as well as opportunities for salt water baths on deck, where the captain had also arranged for a swing to be put up for exercise. There was also the callous (to modern eyes) practice of trying to hook or shoot various seabirds including the albatross, either ignorant or uncaring of the sailors' superstition which was recorded in Coleridge's 'Ancient Mariner.' Concerts were occasionally performed, with some of the passengers or crew taking their turn at singing or reciting, and occasional dances. A weekly newspaper, the Observer, was also produced on board every Saturday. "It alluded to the concert on board the other evening. I was highly flattered, my song having been put down as the 'Gem of the Evening'. We have all to give it our support by becoming correspondents. The captain was asking if the hens killed in the morning was in its obituary of deaths!" Each Sunday morning there was a service taken by Mr Grant (apart from the first day out when the reverend gentleman was laid low with sea sickness), with Alick being asked to act as precentor when he led the congregation in hymn singing.

But on the whole, "eating, reading, and lounging down, are the great things that wear away the long day." He spent a good amount of time reading, and although he remarks that "light reading is the best for on board ships," his choice included Burns, Shakespeare, Scott, Don Quixote, a History of Scotland, a book called 'Noctes Ambrosianae' which described imaginary conversations between the Edinburgh elite of the 1820s, and 'Olney Hymns,' a collection of inspiring verses by John Newton and William Cowper. Perhaps these books did represent light reading in Victorian times.

Although his mind must have been set on his new life to come, there were occasions on board when Alick was overcome by homesickness. Three months before he left Glasgow, he went back to Gigha with his sister to say goodbye to his family; and "occasionally I take up my album and see all your dear faces there before me – your very images, and I wish you only knew the comfort I derive from that book." On the thirteenth day out, he stood "behind the man at the wheel thinking of dear friends. I was conscious that every passing hour was taking me miles and miles further away from you all and then I could not help thinking to myself 'How is this?' and 'Will I ever see them all?'"

Shipboard customs which were common to most ships of the time were recorded faithfully. "In emigrating this way, sailors have an old custom of bringing you in for a bottle of rum, if they catch you up in any part of the rigging. Although aware of this I was anxious to see a second sunset by going aloft, so I went up the rigging of the mizzen mast and I was not many steps up when I was hotly pursued by one of them. He of course fixed me with a rope but loosed me as soon as tied – I all the time delighted. When I came down I gave him a bottle of the 'desired stuff'. You are quite at liberty to go up the rigging as often as you like after being once caught."

Crossing the equator was the classic occasion for enjoyment. "The sailors of course asserted that Neptune came on board. Two of them dressed up supposed to be Neptune and his wife (God and goddess of the sea). They did their part very well – having shaved five of the sailors who never crossed before with tar used for soap, after which they were all immersed in a large tub of water, head foremost – how we all laughed. We all had to pay tribute (viz a bottle of rum) – music and dancing was kept up till a later hour. The whole performance of Neptune was most capital. It is certainly a great affair crossing the Line, some ships take no notice of it, but our captain does not go against it."

Alick had an excellent eye for observing his fellow passengers and their characteristics, understandable in such confined conditions, and as he noted: "I don't think there is any place that can show everyone's mind or character so well as on board ship, the limit being so small." At first he got on well with the doctor – "such a nice little long red-whiskered fellow" – though not the doctor's wife, but later in the voyage they both fell from grace. The Baptist minister also declined in popularity on board – "no-one cares for his company" – possibly due to his prejudice against dancing and general enjoyment. His two particular friends on board were Mr Sanderson (whom he travelled out with) and Mr McKellar: no first names in those Victorian times.

There were a few moments of very gentle flirtation on both sides: "I gave a sixpence today to a youth (aged about 10) for kissing one of the Misses Roberts whilst asleep in her chair on the poop – this is a usual thing, when the lady is caught sleeping by the heat of the sun – and she herself is required to present a pair of gloves. The boy did it very smartly and was the cause of great applause." The next evening (presumably by way of retaliation): "I was reading all alone at the table at the saloon when I was disturbed by biscuit crumbs scattering all around me. It did not take long to conjecture whence they came from; I kept quiet however and next came down on the top of my head a Ladies hat (let down by a cord) which I instantly snatched and locked up – shall deliver it to the young lady when I see fit."

But for most of the time, as a man of his generation, he had a chauvinistic approach to the ladies on board who (not surprisingly) were prone to sea-sickness and found conditions on ship trying and often alarming. "We are very much annoyed with one of the Misses Roberts whose mind is so timid at night, expecting to see the ship go down, and when she sees a flash of lightning she rushes into her cabin in a state of great distraction." Although he envies the ladies for their ability to pass the time by sewing and knitting, he eventually gets "perfectly tired of the ladies titter-tattering." By the end of the voyage, even the captain is becoming annoyed with them for asking him for the exact time they will sight land. Five days before landing, Alick's shrewd eye was taking in their preparations for landing: "Our ladies on board are commencing to undo their fashions laid up carefully in their boxes during the voyage. It is for me most amusing to see them all consulting with each other "how this" and "how that" will look. I asked one of them today if she had fixed yet upon what style of chignon she would wear on stepping ashore."

As landfall drew near, the crew were hard at work freshening up the ship after her stormy passage: "all over our ship has been painted white, and everything looks so fresh and clean." There was a sweepstake (tickets three shillings each) operating on which day they would land, with the head steward holding the stakes. Thanks to a combination of fresh winds and the skilled navigation of Captain Watson and his crew, the trip took 73 days from land to land, "the quickest of this season's ships," to the great satisfaction of the Captain. It was no wonder that Alick headed the penultimate entry in his diary with "Land, Land Ho!!! and I need not tell you that I am filled with gratitude to God for that blessed sound," when Cape Otway and Port Phillip Heads outside Melbourne were finally sighted.

The end of Alick's story is a sad one: he died just two years after reaching Melbourne at the age of 23 from tuberculosis, that scourge of the times which also took the lives of his two brothers and a sister. So his long journey, taken with such optimism and courage to his brave new world, was cut tragically short. He died alone and unmarried at his accommodation in Highett Street in Melbourne's borough of Richmond, and was buried in an unmarked grave in Boroondara cemetery. He never did get back to Gigha to see his family again: when his father died four years later, his mother added Alick's name to his father's headstone in the peaceful Kilchattan graveyard in Gigha. It is some comfort to know that, thanks to his journal which was written under the billowing sails of a clipper, his words still ring out fresh and clear some 140 years after he left his native Scotland.

My Diary

London to Melbourne in Ship *Macduff*, Captain Watson

Note: Long and Lat are as at 12 o'c each day. Total run is for the last 24 hours up to 12 also.

1st day. Sunday 18th April 1869

Yesterday evening our Pilot left us off Isle of Wight and took with him my last Despatches for home and other friends. This is my first Sunday at sea. In the morning rose at 8 and after dressing went up on Poop. Far behind is still to be seen the Lizard Point and Devonshire Coast. Up to 12 noon we had a favourable breeze, after which it stilled down for a perfect calm till about 3 when again a smart breeze got up and made our ship go 8 knots. The passengers (especially the ladies) have enjoyed the Poop all day sitting on chairs reading with rugs, plaids, and all comforts round them. We had no Divine Service on board today on account of our parson (Mr Grant) suffering from sea sickness caused by the ship 'pitching' all last night. All round us are ships outward bound like ourselves, but I fear time and speed will soon make us dispense with each other. This day has been altogether very pleasant, neither too cold nor too hot. We had for dinner the following dishes, viz: 1st choice of all soups, Roast beef, roast mutton, pork, Australian beef and fowls, 3rd rice, sago, Black Cherry and many other puddings and pastry, 4th bread and cheese, 5th Fruit consisting of apples, oranges, figs, raisins, almonds nuts etc etc served up in the saloon. So much for our every day's dinner on board, by which you will perceive we are not meant to starve. I may state that our meal times are Breakfast at 9, Luncheon at 12, Dinner at 4, Tea at 7 and Supper at 9.30. All lights are out at 10.30 at which hour I retired.

2nd day. Monday 19th April

Our sailing is reckoned from this day. After dressing got on Poop at 8.30 and walked about for half an hour. We are now into the ocean and all the eye can see is one ship and a large steamer, both very far distant. We have been steering West all day in the strong breeze from SW by S. Our average speed today is 7 knots. After tea rain fell which prevented my going on Poop. Towards night the wind veered round more to the south which will carry us well out. I witnessed for the first time the 'log glass' being used, which is kept up before the eye while the line is being thrown over, thereby testing the ship's speed. I enjoyed myself studying 'Shakespeare' in my hammock most of the day. I must now give you an idea of my berth. It is on the starboard side, enters from centre of saloon, and half as large as an ordinary bedroom. There are two sleeping berths. The lower one is occupied by my good friend Mr Sanderson from Edinburgh who is going out to the Colonies for the improvement of his health, and the top one is my property. The port hole is right above my knees in bed and this I take care to open in the mornings and shut at evening, just as you would one of your bedroom windows at home. On the floor is a new carpet and at the door a crimson mat, the latter uncommon and quite a novelty on board. On either sides are our trunks, in the corner the wash stand and above is a long shelf for books etc. All round we have fixed brass knobs for our coats and hats. The mirror graces the centre nailed against the wall and under which hangs our combs and brushes. Everything we have got 'ship shape' and warranted perfect fitness. I have now given you a picture of my cabin with which I shall end up my 2nd day's diary.

Lat 49.27N Long 5.21W Total run 106 miles

3rd day. Tuesday 20th April

We have had very favourable weather all this day, wind blowing strong from the SW and are going due south at rate of 9 ½ knots an hour. At breakfast this morning our Head Steward was by the 'pitching' of the ship thrown through the door into Mrs Grant's cabin. We have seen no vessels today. The ladies are now making their appearance after suffering very much from sea sickness. Our Second Steward has also, since we left England, experienced that pleasure, and is not yet able to assist at table. Towards night the sea ran high and caused the ship to heave and roll tremendously. It is with great difficulty that I can walk from my cabin door to the other end of the saloon. I have not been very much on the Poop today, having coiled myself in my hammock reading.

Lat 48.21N Long 6.13W Total run 147 miles

4th day. Wednesday 21st April

The sea around us this day has been as smooth as glass with a very heavy swell, and we have been quite becalmed since morning. The day is pleasant and refreshing with a warm sun. We are now getting into the Bay of Biscay, but saw nothing of the "French coast" and may possibly reach Melbourne without seeing any land. We have not moved all this day – rather monotonous life, but I trust we may get some wind to push us on soon. Our sails have been flying back and forward all day and the rolling of the ship is enough of shake her frame and masts asunder. This has been a glorious day on the Poop. Had a long conversation with a Mrs Cameron who has been repeatedly to Australia. This lady was a fellow passenger with Mr and Mrs Mal. McNeill (brother of Col McNeill late proprietor of Gigha) coming from Melbourne some years ago in the Great Britain and is a relation of the McKellars, Glenreasdale, Kintyre. There are two nephews and a niece with her on board (McKellars). Enjoyed 'Burns' a good deal since morning. At dusk have been favoured with a slight breeze and we are going WSW making about 7½ knots.

Lat 45.53N Long 5.48W Total run 138 miles

5th day. Thursday 22nd April

Last night's breeze did not continue long. We are again becalmed all this day and quite motionless, except that 'rolling' so common to the Bay of Biscay. Was up on the Poop all evening playing at quoits on deck and other games. The former seems a great favourite on board all ships and is joined in by all the ladies. I spent half an hour firing with a falcon pistol at empty bottles, thrown overboard by the Stewards. The owner of it afterwards fixed a piece of paper high up between two ropes (main brace) and commenced firing when he was desperately attacked by the Captain, who declared such a small action might be the means of putting his mast overboard by the breaking of these two ropes. The pistol was soon put out of sight and I dare say won't re-appear in a hurry. About 8 o'clock this evening a steamer passed 5 or 6 miles off bound from Lisbon to Ireland. Our Captain thought another vessel was seen afterwards going in same direction, but it was nearly 10 o'clock. At the time their lights only could be seen. These steamers we all envy in this calm weather. Tonight closes without a breath of wind and the stars and moon are all beautifully seen.

Lat 45.13N Long 5.48W Total run 105 Miles

6th day. Friday 23rd April

We have quite a change this morning. The weather is very favourable, wind being fair, and we are going pretty fast steering WSW. The Captain thinks we are too far in land and wishes therefore to go as far west as possible. At 11.30 we were graced with the presence of a whale which followed us by our side for fully ten minutes then bound its way northwards. A large steamer with part sails up has been sighted ahead all day going in same direction. We could not keep pace with her engines as the wind was not strong enough for our outspread wings. She gradually disappeared after being in sight all day. The rotundity of the world struck me very forcible today as that steamer sunk from view – first her hull, then her funnels, and gradually her top masts. It was indeed a pleasing sight to me. Our chief officer a Scotsman has very kindly been demonstrating a little navigation to me from off his chart, showing me how to take my own Long. and Lat. I must not forget to tell you that I have the charge of the clock above mirror in the saloon, having before leaving London expressed my wish to keep it wound up, during voyage – all of course to occupy time and to make myself as near home as possible. Our speed all this day has been fully nine knots. We have this evening passed within 187 miles of Cape Finnistere in Spain. Little did I think when committing that Cape to memory at school that I should now be so near it. The Captain joined us in playing at quoits. This fair wind puts him in such good humour. I like him very much especially at the Table. I joined the company tonight in the saloon playing at cards. All the ladies (except the parson's wife) strange to say have been to the Colonies before; this however does not prevent them getting sick when the ship ploughs her deck in the waves. We have been amused tonight looking down on the second class passengers' amusements from the Poop, which place is my great favourite spot on board. I shall now I think close this day's diary. They have all retired except myself and the ship's lights in the saloon here are about to be extinguished.

Lat 44.19N Long 8.47W Total run 77 miles

7th day. 24th April

Weather bright and charming. Sun very warm and again we have fair wind. This has been the most beautiful day I ever saw. There were two ships in sight before noon, one homeward bound, the other making for the Straits of Gibraltar. This is a jolly day and we are going round the world flying. I wish this weather would continue for it would soon bring us to the 'Line'. From yesterday at 12 o'clock till 12 o'c today has been the best run we have had yet. I may tell you that the weather hitherto being as fine I have dressed on board just as I would going to Church at home. Our ship is now fairly out of the Bay of Biscay and I can assure you am not a bit sorry for its constant swell was enough to make anyone deranged. Have been reading 'Don Quixote' on Poop yesterday and today and occasionally taking a walk with the Doctor who is such a nice little long red whiskered fellow and has been to the Crimea and other foreign parts. I prefer his company to any on board but I always have more conversation with a Mr McKellar (an Australian about 19) than with any other. This latter is going out along with a sister and brother to their parents who reside 200 miles from Melbourne and they have been in Scotland for the past 5 years receiving Education.

We are not going quite as fast as yesterday as the breeze is lighter. There is always great anxiety evinced every time the log is thrown, to ascertain our rate of sailing and at noon of each day to know our daily run and our precise locality on this vast terraqueous globe. At the present time I would be loathe to leave my 'Ocean Home' for the best paradise under the sun. Everything seems so charming today. I have just had tea and it is now getting dark. It is a curious fact that one on board likes jams or jellies to tea, so that little luxury is, and must be, specially put down for one. Our different roasts and joints at dinner etc vary much so that I don't think we have had two dishes alike since leaving Gravesend; indeed if you prized a <u>certain</u> dish very much, it would be a chance to get a repetition, such is the variety of good things on board and I must say the cooking is of the best and their daily puddings I like exceedingly well. We get meat to Breakfast, again at Luncheon, also at Tea same as Dinner. Potatoes find their way pretty easily off the Table at Breakfast, rather an unusual dish, but a general thing on board ships. I must stop this talk and can't help again adverting to the loveliness of the past day. My first week's observation is nearly coming to an close and will now put past my Diary and will wait to see what tomorrow (Sunday) brings forth.

Lat 44.28N Long 11.10W Total run 191 miles

8th day. Sunday 25th April

We have had service on board at 10.30 (Revd. Mr Grant) and the bell rung forward same as a parish Church. Our parson being a Baptist disapproves of such forms. You will be amused when I tell you that a deputation waited on me shortly after breakfast praying that I should act as Precentor. I scarcely knew at first what to say, so I told the person who was the keenest, to go all round and if he was beat that I would not see him at a loss; as I suspected such was the case and I of course had to perform the task and managed it wonderfully with perfect coolness. Now that the parson has got the ice broken I will have to lead our psalmody every Sunday until we reach Melbourne. You will be saying now that I am being promoted at sea.

We have had to tack against the wind all day but that makes very little difference as our ship with plenty of wind can go within 5½ points of the wind. All the sailors have to appear clean mustered on deck every Sunday. We made two long tacks today and I may tell you that after she rounds it takes the sailors fully an hour to shift and rectify everything. There is very little difference on board from other days.

Lat 39.28N Long 13.54 Long Total run 159 miles

9th day. Monday 26th April

Nothing could be more desirable to us than this day. Breeze is strong and favourable. We have overtaken two ships ahead and passed them both, such is the *Macduff*'s speed, and her Captain assures us that all know her by this. One of the ships we signalised as going to Australia like ourselves. A shoal of porpoises followed us today for nearly an hour. We are this evening about the Lat. of Gibraltar, but would be much further on had we not been becalmed for two days last week.

This morning when I rose I was troubled <u>with a sore headache</u>, the results of reading too long on Poop last night, and it has lasted all day, but am much better tonight. The two ships we overtook and passed are tonight miles behind us. I am sure they will both be grievous at our speed which has been much of day 10 knots.

I wish to let you know that the colour of the water here is of a deep blue black – quite different from what surrounded us at home. As for the sky it is of a beautiful blue with white clouds – no dark smoky looking clouds to be seen here. One thing surprises me that the eye (to my opinion) cannot reach so far in the ocean, for if a ship is seen 10 miles off only the masts can be seen. Walked from 8 to 9 this night with Mrs Cameron and her niece Miss McKellar who are the nicest of all the ladies on board. I may tell you at once that the Doctor's wife (who sits opposite me at table) I dislike very much. She is a good specimen of her tribe, viz., Yankee. The moon's coming forth tonight was to me a very glorious sight.

Lat 37.20N Long 14.11W Total run 177 miles

10th day. Tuesday 27th April

The wind is W and very slight. Bay most agreeable and cool. There has been two ships to our lee all day, the *Cabot* and *Furnace Abbey* both bound for Australia. We left them 3 miles behind before teatime. I played at quoits for an hour in the forenoon. The sky today is nearly all blue. We noticed at 3.30 (just as the bell rang for us to dress for dinner) a large turtle by our ship's side, which, the Captain concluded, must have wandered away from some shore. We tried to catch it for the sake of delicious soup, but failed. There is no swell or rollers now, and today the wind being very slight, there is not a ripple on the water, just a day you often see at the coast in July. It is nice for us when we have ships in sight and altho' 12 miles off can speak to each other by that wonderful apparatus – flags and ensign. You will I fear think my diary too curtailed, but to save prolixity I must be as concise as possible. Our doctor's little daughter let her hat fly overboard today. At table it is so amusing to hear her Yankee Mamma (who has got the largest hands I ever saw on womankind) ask for some more cheese "please for my Lilly" who drinks as much 'stout' as her Father or Mother.

Lat 34.49N Long 15.23W Total run 168 miles

11th day. Wednesday 28th April

Land! Land! called out to me. Since early this morning till 2 pm. We have been sailing past quite close to Madeira (west side). Being only 4 miles off we could see with our telescopes (which are very numerous on board) everything on shore. Now I will give you a description of the Island which I understand is very much frequented on account of its mild and equable climate. There are a good many townships (curious looking detached houses) and the Island itself is 35 miles long I should say, rises very abruptly out of the Atlantic and the mountains are higher than ever I saw, and near the shore are very precipitous rocks. This Island produces the famous wines known by its name. We could see while passing the vineyards high up <u>on the hills</u>. I was so glad when I awoke this morning to see Madeira thro' my porthole as we saw nothing of land since leaving England. The delight imparted by the first sight of land can only be appreciated by those who have been for weeks at sea, with nothing to meet the eye, day after day, but the same monotonous and dreary circles of water. We were for 2 hours becalmed off Madeira in the forenoon, but all day since have had a nice breeze with us. Outside of us we signalised the ship *Mayoress* from the Clyde to Trinidad 19 days out. We saw a good many small boats rowing between us and the Island, which we thought were coming with fruit to sell, but they did not come near us. The town of Funchal (a glimpse of it we only saw) is on the South Coast and exports much wines I am told.

We are now this evening long past Madeira, soon will lose sight of it, and in a day or two may possibly see the Canary Islands (i.e.) if we do not go too far west. What a lovely day this has been, and not too hot. We shall however very soon have the tropical sun burning down upon us. A sort of concert has commenced on board tonight at 8. Penny readings, songs etc. They put Capt. Watson in the chair. I for my share gave 'The Anchor's Weighed' a song which all thought very applicable, and particularly well sung hear! hear! As I know you would like to see the programme here is a copy.

Programme

Reading 'Mary Queen of Scots' Mr McKellar

Song 'The Cavalier' Mr Bourne

Reading 'Tom Sawyer's Party' Dr Mason

Song Mrs Hammond (2nd class passenger)

Song 'The Anchor's Weighed' Mr Macneill

Reading 'Burns' address to the de'il' Capt. Watson

Song 'Fifty Years Ago' One of the sailors

Recitation. Do

Above came off very satisfactorily indeed and occupied an hour and a half.

Lat 32.49N Long 17.14W Total run 125 miles

12th day. Thursday 20th April

Fair wind all day but very little of it, however, it is better than a calm. I am not able to give my remarks on the weather, but that it is such another day of pleasure as yesterday. The awning has been put up above our heads for the first time on the poop and it makes the atmosphere so much more cool and agreeable. One vessel only is in sight today and outward bound. We have not been fortunate enough to speak with any coming home, but will likely meet with some in the tropics and if I can, shall drop you a word or two in the shape of a letter (i.e.) if we shall find any ship willing to carry our letters. As you are aware before we get to Melbourne we shall lose about 10 hours time and therefore are losing every day. Some on board alter their Watches at 12 o'clock daily, but I shall not touch mine but allow it to take its course for this reason that I think it injurious to all chronometers.

Lat 31.10N Long 19.30W Total run 136 miles

13th day. Friday 30th April

"Where do you think we are now?" said the Captain to me when shaking hands that morning. "We have now," says he, "got into the trade winds." Now I must tell you that these winds blow here always in the same direction, viz., from the North, and of course right with us. The breeze is nice and strong today, and we are going at a great pace and won't slacken our speed until we reach the Equator which at this rate will be only 12 days. Such are the advantages of the Trade Winds – I wish you were on board to see the extent of sails set. It is really a very fine sight to stand at the stern and look upwards at our vast wings which are something like a large hill covered with snow. I stood before dinner today behind the man at the wheel and looking back thinking of <u>Dear friends!!</u> I was conscious every passing hour was taking me miles and miles further away from you all and then I could not help thinking to myself "How is this?" and "Will I ever see them all?" After these meditations I came downstairs to my berth and took up my Railway rug which I spread on the poop. Here I laid down and read for nearly 6 hours – what more can I do? Eating, Reading, and Lounging down, are the great things that wear away the long day.

We overtook a large ship this evening, which in the morning was unseen to us. It is just like going over a large hill and to meet with ships on the other side. Our track all this day if traced on a map would be a perfect straight line. This is the last day of spring and it was on the first of it that my sister, and myself, left Glasgow for Gigha. Very long and changeable 3 months they seem to me.

Lat 28.23N Long 22.38W Total run 176 miles

14th day. Saturday 1st May

I now enter on a new month, and this is the first day of summer with you all at home. I can well picture you all going out and speaking of the May dew. I am only sorry that I cannot join you. Do you remember, dear Johnnie, the long walk you and I took before breakfast this day one year, and of the two pence worth of milk we bought from the Dairy woman in or near Partick? These recollections are pleasant now to me, and come up quite vividly to my mind.

Our fair wind and breeze continue, and today is just the same as yesterday. At breakfast we overtook and passed a barque which turned out to be the *Argo* from Cardiff to Table Bay, 20 days out. She is now far behind. As yet we have not met with any at all to come up to our ship for sailing. At 6 o'clock last night the first reading was given from a newspaper just started on board and called the 'Observer'. It is amusing to see the newsreader going round the ship calling 'Observer'! It alluded to the concert on board the other evening. I was highly flattered, my song having been put down as the 'Gem of the Evening'. There is an Editor and the paper comes out every Saturday. We have all to give it our support by becoming correspondents. The newspaper also contains conundrums. Some articles stolen, etc etc, and the Captain on hearing this was asking if the hens killed in the morning was in its obituary of deaths! We also spoke this morning to the *Alarm* from Bordeaux to Buenos Ayres 18 days out.

Lat 25.12N Long 23.13W Total run 167 miles

15th day. Sunday 2nd May

First Sunday of Summer and a lovely day it has been with us on board here. The wind is as fair as it can blow but not enough of it. In the morning we had Divine Service on board on the poop quite in the open air, and we all had our hats off, so you can imagine what weather it is. I of course had again to be precentor. Today I led off first with 'Hursley' (the tune you use for Rock of Ages in your Church at Sandyford, and which I was much attached to).

    Mr Grant chose for his text 'And there was no more Sea', Par XXI and 1 verse. I spent the most of this holy day reading 'Olney Hymns', some of which are very appropriate for me at present. Occasionally I would take up my album and see all your dear faces there before me – your very images and I wish you only knew the comfort I derive from that Book. Now I want to impress upon your mind that at sea you can't relish reading books however infinitely precious the contents of them may be, something or other seeming to fix your mind otherwise, but for all this, I read a good deal but forget the most. Light reading is the best for on board ships. We have seen no memorable things this day except one stormy petrel that skimmed on the waves at our stern for some time. It seems to me like an age since we left Gravesend such is the feeling, but I shall soon get over it. We are now more than 2,000 miles from England.

Lat 22.37N Long 23.12W Total run 167 miles

16th day. Monday 3rd May

I am writing up my day's Diary this evening on the saloon table and the sun is shining in upon me through the cabin window. It is within an hour of tea time. Read a good deal and finished today a novel entitled 'Half a Million of Money' which is very well written indeed. I was all alone on deck with the Captain till a late hour last night. He is such a jolly fellow and tells such curious stories. He summoned all up on deck at 10 last night to see that beautiful constellation which is only seen from the ocean, viz. the 'Southern Cross'. This is four bright stars (which I never shall forget) in the South and very low on the horizon. They form a perfect cross and are a great guide to mariners. After dinner today I laid down in my cabin and pondered over a lot of old letters which made me quite homesick. I am not ashamed to acknowledge this, as I think anyone with a heart at all would be affected likewise. We are having the best possible weather, bracing clear and calm. The sunset was glorious this evening, reflected in the distance from the snow white peaks of those lovely clouds. Tomorrow night I understand a concert is to take place among the second class passengers. No ships seen this day.

Lat 20.38N Long 23.58W Total run 127 miles

17th day. Tuesday 4th May

We are gradually getting into warmer weather now, every day. Today the sun has been extremely hot: when we left England the Therm. showed 59°, it is now 81°. A child let its playing ball fall overboard in the morning, and it being calm at the time the sailors could have rescued it but the Captain at once cautioned them against doing so for fear of the sharks. We have all been keeping a sharp look out for these monsters today but saw none. No one dare go with a little boat this hot weather in case of being attacked by them.

We have seen porpoises and several times to my great delight some exquisite little nautiluses floating on the blue waves a few feet below me, as I lay on the sofa in our cabin. They looked like bubbles or little crystal globes glittering with all the colours of the rainbow. These little creatures are a kind of shellfish and hoist a sail, and the sailors name them 'Portuguese Men of War'. We caught several of them by throwing out a kind of bag with hooped mouth, which one of the ladies made purposely. The breeze of trade winds has died away and we have been all this day becalmed. I fear we shall have a long voyage the weather being so good. We only made 74 miles since 12 o'clock yesterday.

I must now tell you that although this is the first week of the summer we have it dark till 8. The days are getting very short with us. It is a strange life here, so much enclosed in this little world isolated on the sea, but when one can stay on deck, as today, till 8.30 in the fresh <u>breeze</u>, it is delightful, delicious, in fact <u>wholesome idleness</u>. I wish you were with me as I am now beginning to miss you all very sadly. As the Concert does not close tonight till 10 or so, I shall speak of it tomorrow. Till then, I shall say goodbye.

Lat 19.20N Long 24.28W Total run 76 miles

18th day. Wednesday 5th May

Nothing of very great importance has transpired today. The sun has been quite as hot as yesterday, but under our awning on the poop it is delightful. I did not come off the poop last night till 12, having been admiring the stars and the quantity of animalculae in the waters which make them appear like fire in some places. Our Captain explained to me the nature of these small animals, and he can tell by seeing them during the day which night the waters will be phosphoric. The Concert last night was not so successful as the one given by us saloon passengers some nights previous. We have been making 5 knots today. I really wish wind would come to make us move.

5.30 pm. The Cape de Verde Islands have just been sighted. They seem a mere speck of high hills but we shall soon get nearer to them, if so, I shall say something about them. I can assure you, we are all glad to see land.

Lat 18.17N Long 24.50W Total run 71 miles

19th day. Thursday 6th May

We have had a splendid breeze of fair wind all day. Did not see any more of the Cape de Verdes. In the morning saw a barque a long way off. We have been fortunate enough today to see shoals of flying fishes – these when chased by a larger fish get set and fly above the waters. The Doctor and I arranged for a dancing party to take place on the poop this evening at 8, so I enjoyed myself very much. My partner was Miss MacKellar, who was specially chosen for me by the doctor who is a jolly sort of fellow. This young lady who has only finished her Boarding School studies in Cheltenham before coming away is the best dancer among the ladies. We had music from a concertina. I may state our reverend parson goes against this mode of amusement and he and I nearly quarrelled over the matter when discussing it.

Lat 15.52N Long 25.33W Total run 143 miles

20th day. Friday 7th May

The weather has been much the same as yesterday and if this breeze continues we shall cross the line about Wednesday evening. I expect to be up at 5.30 for the first time tomorrow morning as the baths all over the ship are now ready and I do really feel inclined for a good "splash". I have now got the cabin to myself – Mr Sanderson having got permission to sleep in the Captain's room during the hot weather in the tropics here, as the perspiration at night is more than he can well endure. I always sleep with only a very thin sheet over me. Today I took a good deal of exercise on the swing erected by the Captain and which is suspended from the mizzen yard. It is used by the ladies as well – the motion of the ship makes is sometimes rather dangerous. If sailors are called to pull on any rope which may be near me I for one never hesitate to give them a hand – as I cannot have too much exercise on board. I write this at 12 o'clock tonight and have been on deck till now expecting some flying fish to fly on board – a light on the ship's side often attracts them.

Lat 13.18N Long 26.17W Total run157 miles

21st day. Saturday 8th May

The end of a week already! and really I am glad. The time to me now seems to pass away very fast. Was up before 6 and had a capital Salt Water bath. I wish now to tell you that in emigrating this way, sailors have an old custom (which is not yet obsolete) of bringing you in for a bottle of rum, if they catch you up in any part of the rigging. Although aware of this I was anxious to see a second sunset (for this can be accomplished by immediately going up one of the masts) by going aloft, so I went up the rigging of the mizzen mast this evening and I was not many steps up when I was hotly pursued by one of them. He of course fixed me with a rope but loosed me as soon as tied – I all the time delighted. When I came down I of course gave him a bottle of the 'desired stuff'. You are quite at liberty to go up the rigging as often as you like after being once caught. Poor fellows I shall give them another yet, as they work so hard and are only allowed a certain quantity of water daily. We shall have some fine fun crossing the line as the sailors then display their talents in shaving you and similar other tricks.

Lat 10.4N Long 26.46W Total run174 miles

The *Macduff* painted in December 1865, four years before Alick sailed in her, entering Port Phillip Heads near Melbourne. Watercolour painting by George Frederick Gregory (c1815 to 1887) who was a noted Australian marine artist. His other paintings include *HMS Victory* and *HMS Duke of Wellington*; *SS City of Adelaide*; *SS Danderong*; and *Confederate and Union Navy Warships*. His son George Gregory Jnr was also a marine artist. (National Library of Australia)

Upper Dock, Aberdeen Harbour, around 1895, showing three cargo vessels loading or unloading coal. (Aberdeen Art Gallery & Museums Collections)

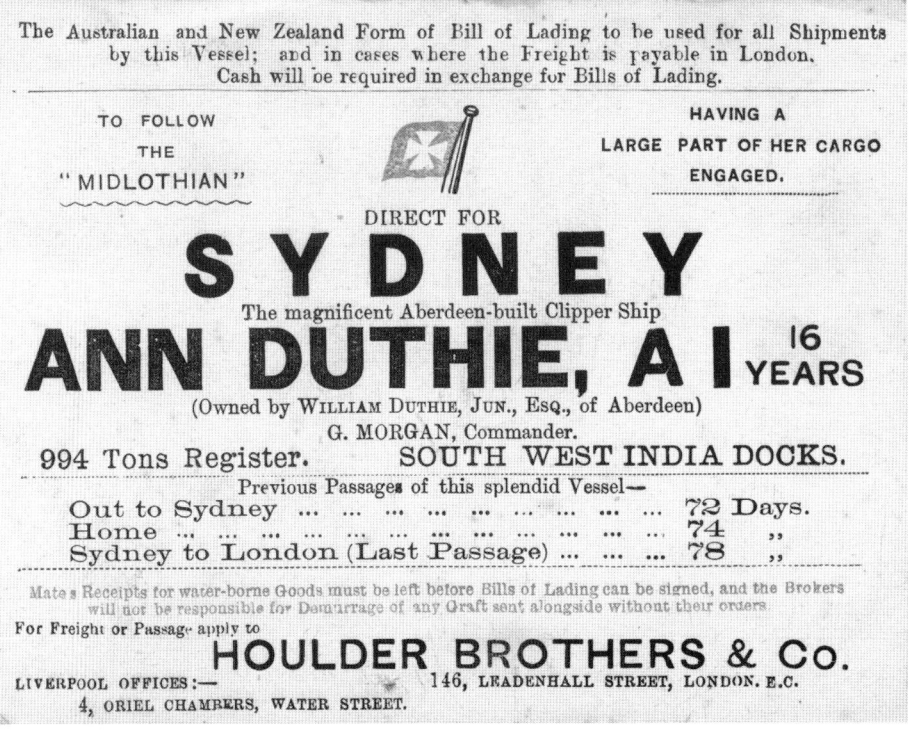

Advertisement for the Aberdeen-built clipper *Ann Duthie* (Aberdeen Art Gallery & Museums Collections)

This 1862 photograph of Alexander Hall and Company's shipyard, Aberdeen, where the *Macduff* was built in 1859, shows the yard's workforce including the owners, master boat builders, carpenters, blacksmiths and (sitting slightly apart on the right) two young office boys. The shipyard is notable for its development of the Aberdeen or clipper bow in 1839. Alexander Hall died in 1849 leaving his two sons James (back row, second right) and William (back, fourth right) to run the business, producing many famous clippers, two of which can be seen under construction. (Aberdeen Art Gallery & Museums Collections)

Possibly the best-known of all the clippers and the last surviving example, *Cutty Sark* was designed by Hercules Linton, a partner in the Dumbarton firm of Scott and Linton. The company, which had never built a ship of this size (963 tons) before, went bankrupt before she was completed. The final fitting out was completed by William Denny and Brothers. *Cutty Sark* was towed to Greenock for final work on her masts and rigging and was launched on 22 November 1869 at Dumbarton on the river Leven.

Her maiden voyage was on 16 February 1870 from London to Shanghai under Captain George Moodie from East Wemyss in Fife. She made eight voyages to China to compete in the races to bring back the new season's tea. The closest *Cutty Sark* came to winning the tea race was in 1872 when she raced *Thermopylae* head to head for the first time, but arrived seven days after her rival due to her rudder giving way.

Cutty Sark is undergoing a major conservation project by the Cutty Sark Trust. She was moored at Greenwich when fire broke out in 2007, but the project work is back on course with the aim of re-opening to the public in 2010.

Painting dated 1993 by Eric F. G. Berryman of the clipper *Thermopylae* built in Walter Hood's shipyard in Aberdeen, preparing to leave Aberdeen harbour on her maiden voyage in 1868. Her first voyage from London to Melbourne was completed in just 60 days. (Aberdeen Art Gallery & Museums Collections)

Jho Sho Maru, built in Alexander Hall's yard, was a barque rigged steamer built for the Japanese Navy in 1868. Although this was a very prestigious order, the firm lost £500 on the project due to a miscalculation of costs. The ship was almost complete when a fire broke out in an adjacent wood store and although the ship was saved from the flames, the yard owner James Hall suffered a fatal heart attack in his anxiety in fighting the blaze. (Aberdeen Art Gallery & Museums Collections)

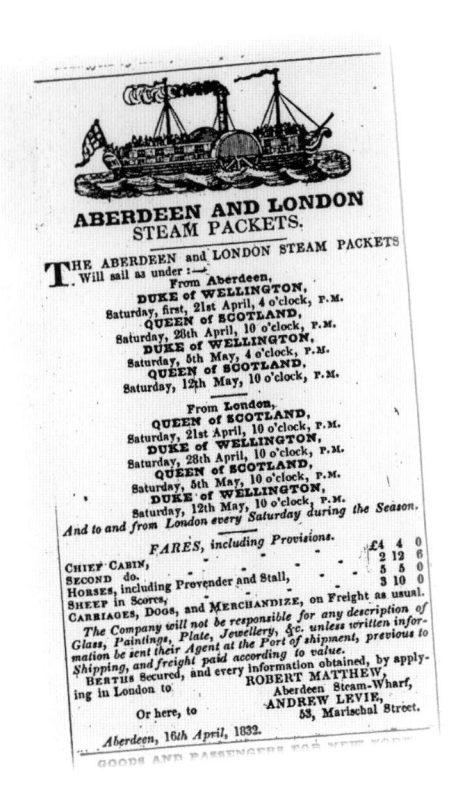

Advertisements in the *Aberdeen Journal* (Aberdeen Art Gallery & Museums Collection)
Macduff passenger list, Melbourne *Argus*, 4 July 1869

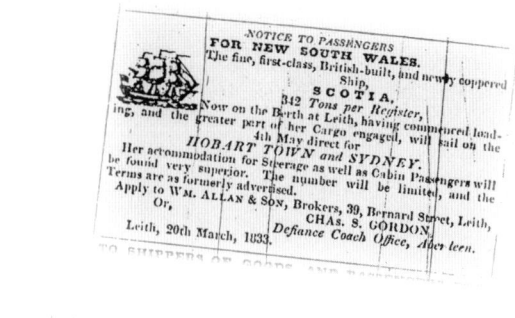

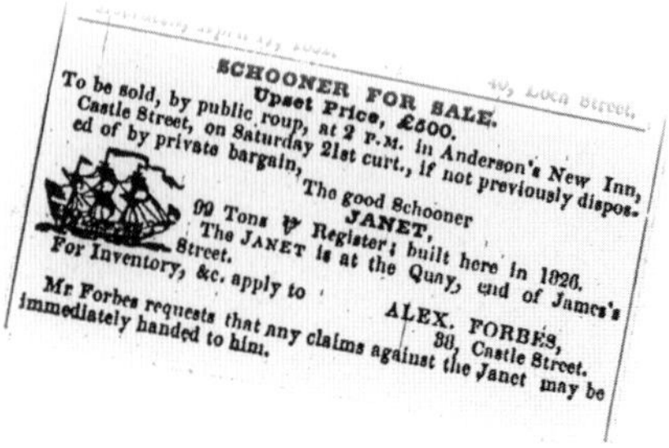

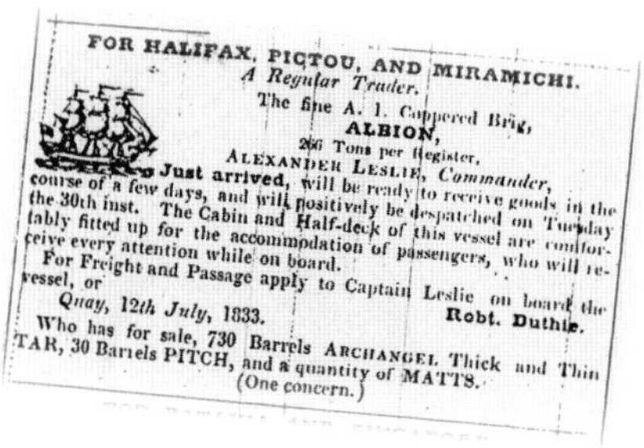

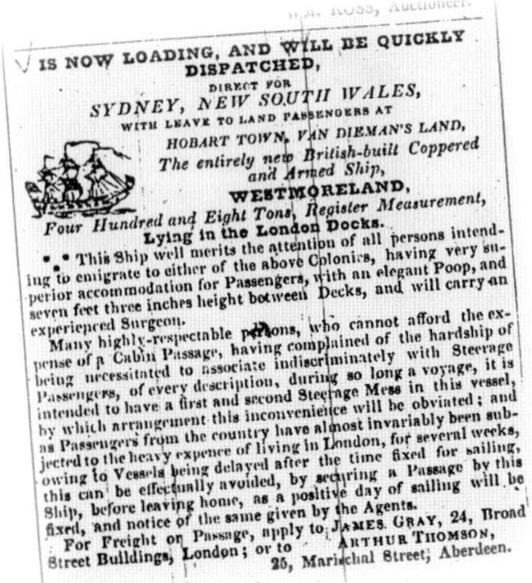

56th Day Saturday 12th June

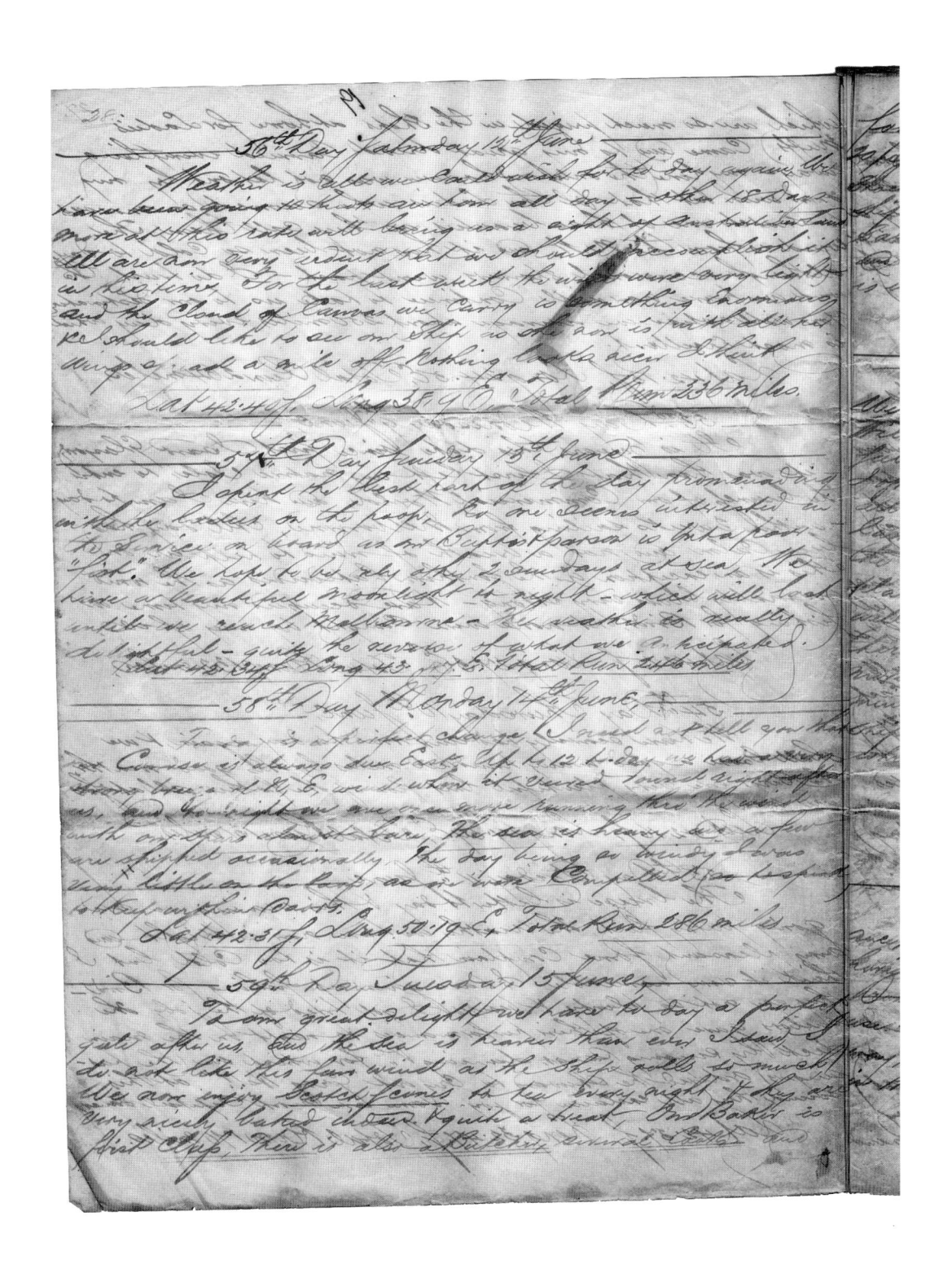

Weather is still a contrary wind for to day again we have been going to the southward all day — other 18 days more at this rate will bring us in sight of Australia I am all are now very anxious that we should see of how it is this time. For the last week the winds were very light and the cloud of canvas we carry is something enormous we should like to see our ship as she now is but we shall keep under a mile off. Nothing to be seen but the ship.

Lat 42.44, Long 38.9 E, Total Run 156 miles.

57th Day Sunday 13th June

I spent the best part of the day promenading with the ladies on the poop. No one seems interested in the service on board as our Baptist parson is but a poor "fish". We hope to have only 2 Sundays at sea. We have a beautiful moonlight to night — which will last until we reach Melbourne. The weather is really delightful — quite the reverse of what we anticipated.

Lat 42.24, Long 43. E, Total Run 246 miles

58th Day Monday 14th June

There is a perfect change I need not tell you that. Course is always due east. Up to 12 to day we had a very strong breeze N.E. wind when it veered round right aft and to night we are once more running thro' the water with every stitch of canvas set. The sea is heavy & a few seas shipped occasionally. The day being so windy I was very little on the poop, as we were compelled for to spend it keeping on our backs.

Lat 42.31, Long 50.19 E. Total Run 286 miles

59th Day Tuesday 15th June

To our great delight we have to day a perfect gale after us. And the sea is heavier than ever I saw it not like this fair wind as the ship rolls so much. We are enjoying Scotch Scones to tea every night they are very nicely baked indeed & quite a treat. Our baker is first class. There is also a Butcher on board

Page from Alick's journal, transcribed on page 47.

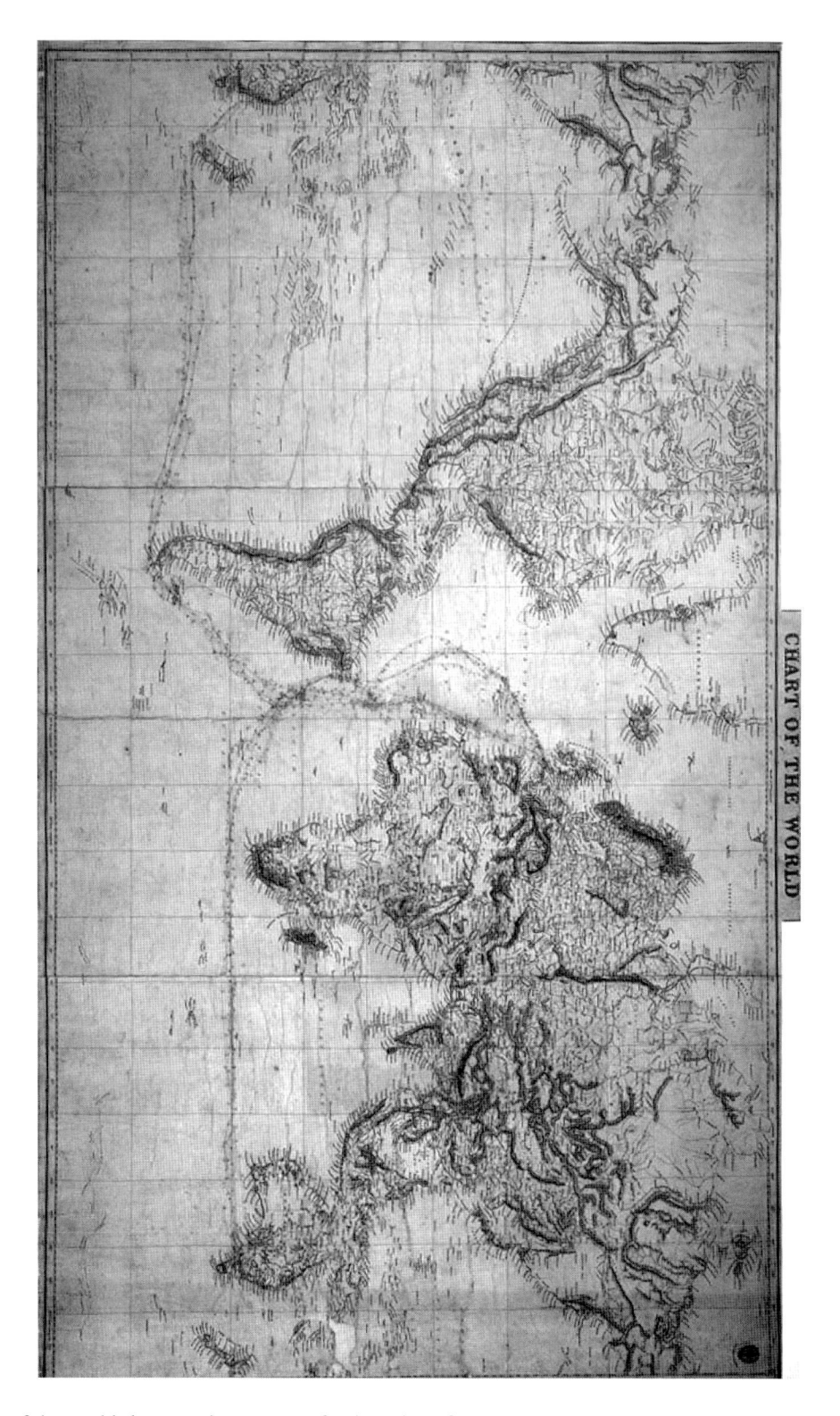

Chart of the world showing the voyages of sailing ships from Britain to Australia in 1874. (Aberdeen Art Gallery & Museums Collections)

22nd day. Sunday 9th May

Have had a most delicious cool breezy day – the sun very warm and wind fast. We had as usual Service on the poop this morning which is attended by all including the sailors. Another flying fish flew on board early this morning and struck our butcher straight in the face. We have seen thousands of them since morning and they fly for a very great distance. Have been reading Sir Walter Scott's works (poems) after dinner. I perspire a great deal since I got up this morning. Indeed everything is now <u>soaking</u> upon me – so great is the heat. I gave a 6d today to a youth (about 10) for kissing one of the Misses Roberts whilst asleep in her chair on the poop – this is a usual thing, when the lady is caught sleeping by the heat of the sun – and she herself is required to present a pair of gloves. The boy did it very smartly and was the cause of great applause.

Lat 8.24N Long 27.0W Total run 125 miles

23rd day. Monday 10th May

We spoke the *Ida Arbacht* (Dutch ship) homeward bound – back to what port we don't know – and she promised to report us on arrival. I was very glad when she hove in sight and I sincerely trust she will be the means of letting you know we are all well so far. It was very possible we shall meet with some more about the Equator (which we shall cross in a day or two). I got one of the sailors today to cut my hair for a bottle of beer, which on board costs 1/- and I feel greatly the better of it. I enjoy a Bath now in the Tropics every morning and it is quite a treat to me – the Captain showed me the sun through this sextant at 12 when right over our heads, but by looking through the instrument the sun is seen going down in the horizon and when the lower part touches the water it is exactly 12 o'c in the day to a second. This is the way the Long. and Lat. are taken at 12 every day. The therm today stands at 94° in the shade. I got one of the ladies (Mrs Cameron) to fix a pugaree round my hat as a protection from the sun which is burning and all on board who had such followed by example. I happened to be reading <u>all alone</u> at the table at the saloon last night about 10 when I was disturbed by biscuit crumbs scattering all around me. It did not take long to conjecture whence they came from; I kept quiet however and next came down on the top of my head a ladies hat (let down by a cord) which I instantly snatched and locked up – shall deliver it to the young lady when I think fit. All this was nicely accomplished from the windows of the sky light above.

Lat 6.7N Long 27.0W Total run 128 miles

24th day. Tuesday 11th May

Have had a nice breeze up till 3 pm when a very heavy shower (a perfect deluge) fell and lasted for nearly an hour – after which it calmed down. These showers are prevalent in the tropics and when accompanied by wind are dismal squalls. Almost all the passengers threw off their Boots and walked about on the wet decks for coolness. It is 4 weeks today since we cleared out of the London Docks and never saw rain till today. The shower was a fine change and caused great sensation. We have seen the polar star, north pole, tonight for the last time and this star I won't see again till I return to Scotland, as it is not seen in the Colonies. I bade it goodbye – so did the

Captain with a wave of his hand. I may state that our Captain is a great astronomer and knows all the stars as well as his ship – when they come in sight and when they will be seen last etc. He can take the time and Lat. from one solitary star.

We are in all 24 cabin passengers – our Parson is a Baptist going out to Tasmania. His wife and children are also with him. He is a great smoker and no-one cares for his company. There are two Misses Roberts who are also going to Tasmania where they hold great property. I believe they are natives of Tasmania. I like them very much as they are very nice companions indeed – always ready to assist in causing Mirth to pass the time. There is a Mr Bourne – fast young man – and has been to all parts of the world. He told me last night he is the cousin of an Earl in England. He is always the cause of great attraction at Table – telling so many curious stories and accounts of the various places he has been to. At table every one keeps his respective place – I sit about the centre and opposite me is the Doctor and wife, at my left the clergyman and suite. A few dolphins were seen at our stern tonight.

Lat 3.58N Long 26.47W Total run 129 miles

25th day. Wednesday 12th May

We have had a tremendous heavy fall of rain after breakfast and the various buckets and dishes are placed here and there to save as much as possible of the blessed element. The showers here are much heavier than ashore, and come and go in an instant. We have a plentiful supply of fresh water on board (chiefly from Melbourne strange to say) but notwithstanding all this, our Captain never loses the opportunity of saving all he possibly can. The allowance to each of us is a gallon a day which comes to our cabin door with boots brushed at 7 o'c every morning. This night has been an amusing one with all the sailors. <u>Neptune</u> is expected on board soon. They very ingeniously formed an imitation horse, mounted it and promenaded round the main deck thrice – followed by a sort of band of their own getting up. The Captain was so pleased that he ordered the steward to give them all a glass of beer. It is quite dark now at 6 and at home you will be all enjoying the long evenings.

Lat 2.56N Long 26.35W Total run 53 miles

26th day. Thursday 13th May

Up till 12 rain fell heavier than ever, rendering it impossible to get out of the saloon – what a change it is to the previous weeks when we were all scorched with a burning sun. My face and hands are all burned quite brown with the sun and another great change is that we have fattened up since coming on board. We end this evening within a few miles of the Equator and the great talk now is about the crossing of it – everyone thinking of the best way of keeping out of the sailors' reach for fear of being shaved or bedaubed with tar. When once you cross it you run clear ever afterwards should you cross it an hundred times. At 12 today St Paul's Rock was 50 miles to our right but too far off for us to see.

Never shall I forget the clouds and sunset this evening – they were so lovely I sat on the poop a long time before tea admiring the beauties of water. I wish you were just with me to see these clouds, only the one half seen other half under the horizon.

Lat 1.03N Long 26.28W Total run 113 miles

27th day. Friday 14th May

This is my Birth Day and it is really a matter of fact ever to be remembered by me that I cross the Equator the day I came of age (if I may so term it). It is a curious coincidence and very few I am sure have the same to say. The hour we crossed the line was shortly before 1 o'c this morning. The Captain, my berth companion and a few more were treated to wine at my expense – I could not possibly let the day pass over without this.

The sailors of course asserted that Neptune came on board. Two of them dressed up supposed to be Neptune and his wife (God and goddess of the Sea). They did their part very well – having shaved five of the sailors who never crossed before with tar used for Soap, after which they were all immersed in a large tub of water, head foremost – how we all laughed. We all had to pay tribute (viz. a Bottle of Rum) – Music and dancing was kept up till a later hour. The whole performance of Neptune was most capital. It is certainly a great affair crossing the Line, some ships take <u>no</u> notice of it, but our Captain does not go against it. Of course the sailors dare not be too harsh without the Captain's consent – everything is under his command. He treated us all in the saloon line to a Champagne Dinner in honour of crossing the Line. We are now in the <u>Southern Latitudes</u> and shall have very long nights. The weather all day has been most charming.

Lat 0.14S Long 26.17W Total run 76 miles

28th day. Saturday 15th May

Being now south of the Equator we shall have very long times at night for many weeks to come. Our course will be shifted in a day, as we have to run due West to catch the trade winds and then come back in the direction of the Cape of Good Hope. This is round about but it must be done to get into those winds. You will understand this nicely by referring to an Atlas with all the Currents shown. About the Cape we expect to run as far South as 44° after which we steer straight for Melbourne. The breeze all this day was pleasant but the great cry is that there is not enough of it. As present we see the moon <u>setting</u> at 9 pm. This is her first quarter (with us) and the shape we see her is like this [crescent lying horizontally] instead of [crescent facing left] as seen in Scotland. In Melbourne I am told she will be of this shape [crescent facing right] – of course it depends altogether from what part of the earth you see her. Early this morning when perfectly dark we nearly ran down a Schooner which chanced to be ahead of us and had no lights up. They seemed to have been all asleep, however our crew saw her and orders were instantly given to 'port the helm' to save collision. One of the sailors has been locked up in jail here for striking our first officer. His mess for the next week to come will be bread and water. We saw four ships today but all too far away. They can be seen from the mast head when we can't see them from the deck.

[No entry]

29th day. Sunday 16th May

This morning just when service was over 2 ships hove in sight (homeward bound) and they passed within a stones throw of our side. We hoisted at once our flags (signalising our name) and desired one of them to report us at Lloyd's which was complied with. This is the second ship that will report us in the papers at home as being spoken with. You have no idea how we all gaze with gladdened hearts at those ships. Have had a better breeze today. I am now getting fully acquainted with all the passengers and spend a great deal of the day walking on the poop with the ladies. Our Doctor and his wife have turned out and proved themselves perfect drunkards – having been both quite intoxicated all last night, disturbing the peace of all passengers. The Captain has given orders to have all liquor kept from them – even at dinner. He (the Doctor) was found with the sailors in the forecastle insensible and uttering seditious language against the ship's Capt and passengers.

Lat 2.31S Long 27.57W Total run 136 miles

30th day. Monday 17th May

There has been a most excellent breeze all day and the *Macduff* is making splendid work. No vessels were to be seen today, although we are at present in the very track of the homeward bound ones. Of course you are aware that ships coming from Melbourne go round Cape Horn and in going out by Cape of Good Hope, thus making a complete circumnavigation. We are only about 250 miles from the South American coast this evening – so far have we come west for the winds but we won't see that land.

Lat 5.22S Long 28.36W Total run 167 miles

31st day. Tuesday 18th May

A strong breeze has been blowing all day with a good sea. We have not had till now (although a month at sea) anything worth calling a right breeze. The *Macduff* has proved now what she can do. She occasionally brings us a good deal of water over the lee side. Notwithstanding all this not one inch of canvas was shortened. At tea tonight it was with great difficulty you could get the cup conveyed to your mouth – some made a nice mess of themselves and others. The Doctor was unfortunate enough to get the contents of his neighbour's cup spilled on his knees. One or two of the ladies are frightened by the ship going so much to one side. The wind is South and we are steering SW by S. At 6.30 this evening two ships hove in sight homeward bound – but am sorry to say it was too dark for us to signalise. It is nearly 11 now and I must "tumble" into Bed and I trust this breeze will last.

Lat 8.19S Long 29.11W Total run 178 miles

32nd day. Wednesday 19th May

All praise is due to the *Macduff*. The wind has been very strong all day and she is going at a fearful pace with as much wind as she can wish for. At home you would call today a half gale of wind but on board here it is treated as the best weather possible and our good ship has still full canvas set. Squalls are very frequent here and when they do come it is very suddenly making us heel over considerably. Mr Sanderson got his hat blown off with the wind this morning. This is really the breeze for us and the Captain is so glad ever and anon muttering to himself "Go on *Macduff*" – so anxious is he to make a quick passage. We fully expected to see some more ships today but none came in sight. You will notice a difference in our total run of each day.

Lat 11.55S Long 29.11W Total run 217 miles

33rd day. Thursday 20th May

The wind is stronger than yesterday and the ocean looks a white foam. We had a very bad squall at 12 which carried away our 'fore royal' to atoms. At 3.30 another struck us quite as strong but no damage done. These squalls last fully 15 minutes. The sail makers are now busy making and replacing the lost sail. A great many birds of the size of a common gull were seen today – brown backed and white breasted – flying very low. A very heavy shower fell in the morning but only lasted 5 minutes. Tonight is beautiful and clear – with large white clouds scudding past the moon. I write with our ship's officer on the poop till past 12. All the rest in bed – watching our ship labouring in the seas. Her speed was 12 ½ knots most of the day.

Lat 15.30S Long 30.38W Total run 230 miles

34th day. Friday 21st May

It has not been quite as windy. Our course all day was due south which is our true calculation. We are now anxiously waiting to see more ships. Games of all kinds are being carried on now on the poop by moonlight – you can read as well as by day light. We expect to be out of the tropics tomorrow night.

    8 pm. Just now a Brig is passing us quite near. We cried "Ship Ahoy!!" and we think they must have heard us. It is quite dark.

Lat 19.30S Long 31.13 W Total run 243 miles

35th day. Saturday 22nd May

We are this evening out of the tropics and no more of the scorching sun will trouble us. The heat all the time in the tropics was intense but not more than can be condoned. For my part I could stand any amount of it. The sailors have been all day up in the rigging as thick as bees, painting and tarring the ropes etc etc. At breakfast time two ships came in sight and passed us homeward bound but too far off for speaking. Breeze all day has been nice and pleasant – no squalls troubled us. Sunset was lovely. Some very beautiful meteors are seen every night falling in all directions.

Lat 23.10S Long 31.13W Total run 213 miles

36th day. Sunday 23rd May

Have been up on the mizzen mast rigging this evening seeing a second sunset. All day has been fine and I may say almost a dead calm. Two ships were seen south east of us but very far off. I am sure you will be pleased to hear that the singing at the Service this Sunday is carried on with great success – under my guidance. This is our 36th day at sea and we have all been remarking that we are now as near as possible half way to Melbourne in point of time but certainly not in distance. After we round the Cape we shall by the gales of wind there make 15 knots an hour.

Lat 25.42S Long 29.45W Total run 174 days

37th day. Monday 24th May

This is the Queen's Birth Day and all the sailors amused us tonight by giving songs and coming forth very tragically, dancing etc. They were rewarded by us all giving them plenty of gin and rum. I have again to say that we are becalmed. A nice breeze sprang up at 10 tonight and it may continue perhaps. Mr Bourne fired at a very large bird in the water but the Captain afraid of a breeze would not allow the jollyboat to be lowered to get it. Our ship carries 2 long boats, 2 life boats and a jollyboat. You would never credit at home that there is such lovely calm weather here. I never go to bed before 12, it is so pleasant sitting up in the poop by moonlight. Mr McKellar and I are always together of course and we always sit up after the rest retire. Indeed I do not know what I would do without him.

Lat 26.24S 27.15W Total run 53 miles

38th day. Tuesday 25th May

I may remark that sometimes I write the original jottings of my Diary lying on the first crosstrees of our mizzen mast. It is a favourite place of mine and forms a nice table to lie down on. Today was very pleasant to us all. The breeze was very pleasant and in our favour. Today was the Captain's Birth Day and we all drank his health with champagne and had a regular jollification over it. A large ship crossed our stern tonight at 10. I witnessed this Evening what is seldom seen and never at all from land, viz, the sun moon and a star all at the same time.

Lat 27.26S 28.54W Total run 63 miles

39th day. Wednesday 26th May

A most splendid fair wind has been blowing all day affording a speed of 10 knots. We do not expect any more calm weather – on the contrary, the passage from the Cape will be rather rough. There has been a very large ship sailing to our lee all day going in the same direction and we are same bound either for Melbourne or Sydney. We may see her again tomorrow morning.

Lat 29.37S 26.59W Total run 170 miles

40th day. Thursday 27th May

If all goes well we expect to be in Melbourne 30 days hence. What a long journey! I must now give you the exact average distance which is 13,300 miles. Rain fell very heavy sometimes, the wind was very strong and right after us causing a very dark sea. Our spanker had to be "scandalised" and all our staysails and studding sails taken down. We saw the first albatross at 3. This is a large bird (seen only at the Cape) and very large. Our Chief Officer informed me today that he once saw one 18 feet – from the tip of the one wing to the other. They are something like the herring gull, but much larger. We hope to get some by the use of gun and bullet. Another large bird here is the Cape Hen.

We were making about 12 knots this forenoon, I can scarcely now write, the ship is rolling tremendously. I wish you saw the scenes at table sometimes. Dishes flying in all directions. There is always fixtures on the table to prevent as far as possible the breaking of dishes.

Lat 32.56S 23.49W Total run 258 miles

41st day. Friday 28th May

A fresh gale blew all day. We were all trying to catch albatrosses and other Birds by lines and strange to say I was the only one successful. The bird I caught is a Cape pigeon and I gave it to the Doctor's wife as I saw she looked at it with a long envious eye. Our 3rd mate, poor wretch, has got intoxicated and created great disturbance. The Captain has put him in chains as he attempted to Commit Suicide by jumping overboard. Tonight is very cold. I must now tell you we are sailing under short canvas, our Royals and staysails being down. All last night was very windy and squally especially at 11, when a very heavy squall struck our ship, which made our Captain jump on deck like a spark of fire. This evening brings us to the Latitude of the Cape of Good Hope. What a long distance south! I can scarcely believe I am as far away from you all.

Lat 34.20S 20.57W Total run 212 days

42nd day. Saturday 29th May

We have not done much progress today. The rolling was tremendous. All the passengers had lines out for birds, but only two were caught. Albatrosses were very plentiful – they are such beautiful animals and fly within a few yards of our ship. The breeze was not very strong today, I think it curious that we have got into cold weather all at once. Vast barriers of ice only exist to the South of us. They are often dangerous in coming round Cape Horn but not here as they are more than a thousand miles from us.

Lat 34.43S Long 19.24 W Total run 82 miles

43rd day. Sunday 30th May

A tremendous sea has been running all day. The wind (a perfect gale) is as fair with us as it can blow and our ship is going at a furious pace. I pity anything that comes across her bow, she rolls very much and very often brings in water on both sides. The main sails are reefed and I may say we are running with bare spars. All the ladies are at various levels of wretchedness. I enjoy the scenery of waves first rate – of course I never saw waves till now – they do truly run as high as many hills, and standing on the poop you would think they could be touched by stretching out your hand. The scene at dinner I shall never forget. Dr Mason who sits opposite me carved the Yorkshire ham and it being a huge size it commenced to roll. I was dressed in my best (to keep pace with others) and I had my eye on it. As I expected down it came <u>with a bang</u> towards me and having my knife and fork in hand I stuck both in it and thereby saved my clothes. This was the cause of great laughter all round.

Lat 37.6S   Long 17.40W   Total run 164 miles

44th day. Monday 31st May.

Although yesterday was a fair specimen of a Cape of Good Hope gale, today is as fine as we could wish for. We passed within 100 miles of the Island of Tristan d'Acunha yesterday and today are not far off Gough's Island. The former rises to a height of 7,800 feet above the sea.

Lat 39.5S   Long 14.22W.   Total run 200 miles

45th day. Tuesday 1st June

If all goes well before the end of this month we expect to see Melbourne. I allow myself to think the time but short now, it is far the best plan. After breakfast I succeeded to the great delight of all in catching an albatross by a piece of pork with hook attached to the end of a long line. When it was brought on deck it proved a monster – all the ladies I saw at once seemed anxious for a muff made out of its breast. The Doctor's wife boldly stepped forward and declared she would have it "<u>if Mr Macneill did not want it himself.</u>" The Captain on seeing this was displeased and threw the bird overboard when at once it flew off not the worse of its hooking. I expect to get another soon. I must tell you <u>that this bird</u> has no power when once on deck of flying off, or from off any hard substance, nor than they rise off the water to fly in calm weather. They bite most fearfully and could snap any one's fingers off.

The breeze has been stiff all day and wind fair. Birds flew high in the air all day and tonight lightning is seen which gives no good sign of the weather. I spent all tonight in the saloon playing at cards with the ladies.

Lat 40.57S   Long 11.8W   Total run 185 miles

46th day. Wednesday 2nd June

I regret exceedingly having to relate that one of the steerage passengers – a short healthy looking man – was washed overboard from off the forecastle poop at 12 o'c. A sailor having seen him ran down to the Stern and threw a life Buoy at him but all in vain. It was blowing a whole gale at the time and has been all day – our ship going 12 knots an hour. 3 sailors jumped into the jolly boat (or dinghy). Helm was put <u>hard down</u> by the Captain's orders. The wind being right after us and the sea running nearly mast high our ship (in the coming round) planted all her jib down in the waves at one pitch and was in danger of being swamped – seeing this and that it was utterly impossible for a small Boat to master such waves our Captain deemed it advisable not to risk the lives of men in such weather and as he himself said they would be engulfed in an instant. This will cast a gloom all over the ship.

All last night it blew very strong; three of our headsails were carried away into ribbons. All today we have been running with a gale of wind and only 9 sails set – 3 to each mast.

Lat 41.35S Long 5.12 W Total run 271 miles

47th day. Thursday 3rd June

All today has been fine and not so much wind till 10 tonight when a gale of North East wind came on. I was tonight on the poop till 12 nearly, and gave the sailors a hand at pulling down the sails. I could scarcely keep my hat on, the wind blew as strong as ever I felt. At 12 o'c today you will notice we were only 1°31" from the Long. of Greenwich so this evening our time here is exactly the same as the <u>Greenwich</u> Observatory. As we go direct East after this our time will gain about 25 minutes a day (or 4 minutes for every degree) so that before we reach Melbourne there will be a difference of 10 hours nearly between your time and ours. The sun is the cause of this. When we were in W. Longitude (this evening we are out of it) our time varied the reverse way. The clock of course in our saloon is altered at 12 daily just after the Captain and Chief Officer take the sun with the sextant.

Lat 42.0S Long 1.31W Total run 70 miles

48th day. Friday 4th June

We are now in East Longitude. All last night blew very hard and the Captain was scarcely in bed at all. From my own bed I could hear the officers giving their instructions to the sailors on deck. The roaring sometimes is fearful. All this day has been fine, but very cold. Took a great deal of <u>gymnasium</u> exercise on deck before dinner to warm myself. I think we have gone so far south now as we require. Our course henceforth will be direct East for Melbourne. Most ships do not go further south than 43 or 44 but the further that way the stronger the winds, which they like.

Lat 42.38S Long 4.25E Total run 248 miles

49th day. Saturday 5th June

I can add very little to my log today. We had a kind of fog this morning which reminded me very much of the Scotch mists. It cleared up towards noon. This is the end of another week (so I term them) and I am so glad.

Lat 42.34S Long 7.31E Total run 136 miles

50th day. Sunday 6th June

We have been scudding with a fair breeze all day. The heaviest we shipped yet came this morning when we were at breakfast. It washed all over the poop and the most of the ladies thought we were sinking. For my own part I have more faith in our good ship.

Lat 42.11S Long 12.57 E Total run 238 miles

51st day Monday 7th June

Today brings us into the Long. of the Cape of Good Hope. I am now glad to tell you that we have got the desired weather at last. We have a speed of 12 knots as an average. The breeze which is very strong is beginning now to be steadier and if it continues we still expect to accomplish the voyage in 70 days which is very extra work – 90 days being the average. I am never happier than when we have a gale of wind, then it is a fine sight to see the gallant *Macduff*'s white foam which she sends forth 100 yds before her bows and all round. It would be madness in any steamer to come along side of us for speed. In a right gale we go 16 knots an hour which is equal to 19 miles. I sometimes read in Bed at night until my candle going out stops me, then with my head resting on the pillow I listen to the mighty waves dashing against my port hole right above me.

Lat 42.25S Long 18.19E Total run 233 miles

52nd day. Tuesday 8th June

Although we have been going over 10 knots all day I tried to catch albatrosses. Just after I had my line out with a splendid piece of pork on the hook, one of these monster Birds which are so much prized in the shops at home for ladies (muffs) came and to our great dread carried everything away – my line (the only one) however was not let out by my own wish but that of the ladies who seemed so anxious to snatch one of those beauties as they call them. The wind is from the NW and it has not been so cold today although occasional showers went past. I do trust the wind we have now will continue to take us to our destination. You will notice we average about 250 miles every day which is most excellent.

Lat 42.15S Long 24.5E Total run 264 miles

53rd day. Wednesday 9th June

It is six years this date since first I saw Glasgow – it was then that I first left my native Isle to enter the business of our Commercial World and here I am today – within 3 weeks sailing from Melbourne. All day has been calm and not a breath of wind to help us on. This is an exception in the Southern Latitudes as the wind invariably blows very strong. Have occupied my time in fishing for Birds but none were caught by any of us.

Lat 42.15S Long 27.3E Total run 132 miles

54th day. Thursday 10th June

We have had scarcely any wind today again and we shall loose a good many hundred miles by this good weather. The birds are very plentiful but few of the (feathered) albatrosses are seen.

Lat 42.16S Long 29.59E Total run 131 miles

55th day. Friday 11th June

The breeze is better today and this evening we are going pretty fast. The weather we have now is bright and very pleasant. Some complain that it is too cold but I think it very agreeable. I have given up fishing for Birds – they are not so plenty and besides I got tired of the job. The sailors gave one of their performances tonight on the main deck by singing songs, dancing etc for which we (the passengers) ordered the steward to cry out 'Grog Ho!!' at this sound they all exclaim for joy. Some are most capital dancers.

Lat 42.37S Long 32.47E Total run 170 miles

56th day. Saturday 12th June

Weather is all we could wish for today again. We have been going 10 knots an hour all day – other 18 days more at this rate will bring us a sight of Australian land. All are now very ardent that we should accomplish it in this time. For the last week the winds were very light and the cloud of canvas we carry is something enormous and I should like to see our Ship as she now is with all her wings spread a mile off. Nothing looks nicer I think.

Lat 42.40S Long 38.9E Total run 236 miles

57th day. Sunday 13th June

I spent the best part of the day promenading with the ladies on the poop. No one seems interested in the Service on board as our Baptist parson is but a poor "fish". We hope to be only other 2 Sundays at sea. We have a beautiful moonlight tonight – which will last until we reach Melbourne. The weather is really delightful – quite the reverse of what we anticipated.

Lat 42.34S Long 43.47E Total run 246 miles

58th day. Monday 14th June

Today is a perfect change. I need not tell you that our course is always due East. Up to 12 today we had a very strong breeze of NE wind when it veered round right after us, and tonight we are once more running thro' the wind with our spars almost bare. The sea is heavy and a few are shipped occasionally. The day being so windy I was very little on the poop as we were compelled (so to speak) to keep within doors.

Lat 42.31S Long 50.19E Total run 286 miles

59th day. Tuesday 15th June

To our great delight we have today a perfect gale after us and the sea is heavier than ever I saw. I do not like this fair wind as the ship rolls so much. We now enjoy <u>Scotch scones</u> to tea every night and they are very nicely baked indeed and quite a treat. Our baker is first class. There is also a Butcher, several Cooks and four Stewards. There is precious little of the 30 sheep, 20 pigs and 200 fowls left now. This was about all the livestock put on board at the London Docks. On board a ship they have everything preserved such as Milk, Beef, Salmon, Haddocks, Eggs, Pease, Rhubarb, Damsons, Gooseberries, and all the <u>etceteras</u>, used for our daily puddings. Soup is every day served before dinner.

Lat 42.52S Long 56.8E Total run 263 miles

60th day. Wednesday 16th June

The wind and our speed is today equal to yesterday. We have had very heavy rain since morning. I read Wilson's "Noctes Ambrosianae" all day at the table in the saloon. The ladies employ their time by sewing, knitting etc. I often envy them – for their manual labour – as for me and all the gentlemen nothing remains to do but ever-lasting reading. I am now getting perfectly tired of the ladies titter-tattering. I don't think there is any place, that can show every one's mind or character so well as on board ship – the limit being so small. Here there are for instance so many ideas and opinions – all more or less varying with each other – I say if a person's mind can be drawn out at all, it is on board a ship; but after all I like the life on the ocean wave, where like Lord Nelson

"Our march is o'er the mountain wave

"Our home is on the Deep."

Lat 42.8S Long 61.48E Total run 248 miles

61st day. Thursday 17th June

Last night closed with a very stormy appearance, with great thunder and lightning and the sky about the horizon all round was as black as ink, but this day promises well. We do not now and for some weeks past use side lights at night as in going due East this way, there are never any ships seen – all are going in the same direction – and no danger is enhanced.

Lat 42.2S 66.41E Total run 222 miles

62nd day. Friday 18th June

Another delightful day, although a shower of rain came once or twice. I was trying to catch some Birds for an hour or two and succeeded but in pulling a large one when my line broke, and guess my disappointment. I have skinned a few for the ladies and gave them the breasts, which are all pure white.

Lat 44.51S Long 72.17E Total run 230 miles

63rd day. Saturday 19th June

At 12 o'clock today we were 2945 miles from Melbourne, and I have to say that at this rate we shall be there before we know where we are. However not having a screw or paddles everything depends upon the winds. We accomplished 1745 miles this week, and next week we expect to log more. Another week's distance will, I trust, leave us only about 1000 miles from our port. We gain on Greenwich time fully 25 minutes each day. To interest you, <u>my dear friends</u>, I must now tell you how I can find out your time at home, although so many thousand miles away from you. Well, you will perceive that we are at 12 o'c today 77½ degrees East of Greenwich meridian. Take this number and multiply by 4 (which means that we gain 4 minutes every degree we go East), this will give you 310 minutes, which divided by 60 gives the time we are ahead of you, viz 5 Hours 10 minutes, and before we get to Melbourne (which is in 145° east Long.) our difference with you will be about 10 hours. Hence the cause of Day light with you when night in Australia – in going forth direct Greenwich time never varies.

Lat 42.2S Long 77.30E Total run 230 miles

64th day. Sunday 20th June

Have been running all day with a fine gale and heavy sea – making 14 knots an hour. The sea being so cross a few were shipped – saw a south sea whale at noon, spouting the water ever so high. We are very much annoyed with one of the Misses Roberts whose mind is so timid at night, expecting to see the ship go down etc and when she sees a flash of lightning she rushes into her cabin in a state of great distraction.

Lat 42.16S Long 84.1E Total run 292 miles

65th day. Monday 21st June

This is your longest day with you at home but with us the shortest. It is dark at 4 now. I rejoice to submit to you 300 miles as our total run today. You will I am sure call this good work. We have still a westerly gale right with us and sea very heavy. I was on the poop at 1 o'c when a "crusher" came in washed right over us and broke down into the Saloon thro' the sky lights. The ladies being all sitting round the table got very much frightened. These seas strike the side of our ship sometimes with the force of a Cannon Ball, and makes her whole frame shudder, still I don't count this unpleasant as we are shortening our distance considerably. On the whole we are enjoying splendid sailing weather and a good voyage. We have all the comforts of life on board, and what more can we wish for. As for the weather we are glad to take what comes.

Lat 42.1S Long 90.45E Total run 300 miles

66th day. Tuesday 22nd June

We have now just enough of wind, and do not wish for more. All last night we were going 14 knots and today our speed is not much less. At 1, orders were given "Stand by halyards!" for an approaching squall. On it came like fury, and two men had to go to the wheel. I also along with some of the more able passengers assisted the sailors in slacking canvas. She did go then "just like an evil spirit" as Captain Watson termed it. You must see before you can conceive the power of a ship in the ocean. She goes as steady as a rock. I shall close up this day's Diary now, and trust that this day week will afford us a sight of land. It will be Cape Otway which is the first sight of Australia we shall see.

Lat 44.41S Long 97.31E Total run 302 miles

67th day. Wednesday 23rd June

All last night we experienced very heavy hail showers and strong winds and today the storm is still kept up, as we are going very fast. The wind is nearly south – blowing up from the vast icebergs about a thousand miles to the south of us, which makes the weather very cold. A few Birds were shot by the gun today overhead, but none fell on Deck. It is amusing to see those creatures taking shelter behind the billow of the great waves. To give you an idea of the size of the waves our ship can sail <u>fully</u> on the top of each of them.

Lat 44.4S Long 103.43E Total run 284 miles

68th day. Thursday 24 June

We are now within 5 or 6 days sail of M. As I said on Tuesday, Cape Otway is the first land we shall see, which is 100 miles from Melbourne, after passing it we go through what is called "The Heads" 45 miles nearer Melbourne which is the entrance into Port Philip. We sail up this Port (which is 40 miles wide) till we come to Sandridge Wharf a mile or so from the city of Melbourne and where the good *Macduff* discharges both her passengers and Cargo. No ships of large tonnage go as far up as Melbourne – I have no observations for my Diary today except that we have had the best possible weather, wind and everything in our favour.

Lat 41.8S Long 109.19E Total run 254 miles

69th day. Friday 25th June

Today brings us into the Long. of Western Australia and of course our time at sea now must be very short. There was thunder and lightning all last night and early this morning our second mate was washed by a heavy sea from the stern up to the poop front – a distance of 20 yards. Today is blowing very hard and <u>sea running</u> high. There is only 2 sails set to the mizzen mast, viz the upper and lower top sails – I know now every sail and most of the ropes on board.

Lat 40.57S Long 115.43E Total run 292 miles

70th day. Saturday 26th June

This day brings us a change of weather. The wind has calmed down and the great breakers of yesterday and previous days have passed away. We are now about 1000 miles from Melbourne and I don't know if we will <u>manage</u> to land next Wednesday evening as we expect, however time will tell. As today is so fine all the sailors are at work scraping the Masts clean, painting the Poop etc so we shall enter Melbourne with quite a brilliant appearance. We have run 2004 miles this week. This will give you an idea of the *Macduff*'s <u>speed</u>. Her <u>sailing</u> qualities are unexcelled I believe by any ship afloat.

Lat 40.16S Long 121.53E Total run 280 miles

71st day. Sunday 27th June

All day has been lovely but rather too little wind. The weather is getting much warmer now as we approach the Australian coast. We are all computing the time now that we shall sight land, and the Captain is quite annoyed by the ladies asking him for the precise minute. Our Parson for one is in a great state to get ashore. I finished the History of Scotland today which I have been studying for the past week or so. I write this at <u>6 pm</u> and at this moment you are all sitting down to Breakfast at Home. This I can see and believe clearly – having come from the Northern to the southern hemisphere. Today we are nearly 13,000 miles away from you.

Lat 39.44S 126.50E Total run 230 miles

72nd day. Monday 28th June

There has been slight showers today, more resembling Scotch Mist. Our speed now only averages 8 knots an hour compared with 15 knots all last week. Our ladies on board are commencing to undo their <u>Fashions</u> laid up carefully in their Boxes during the voyage. I suppose they shall all come out strong on landing. It is for me most amusing to see them all consulting with each other "how this" and "how that" will look. I asked one of them today if she had fixed yet upon what style of chignon she would wear on stepping ashore, and whether or not it was made up. Let me here remark <u>a fact</u> that this Lady was deprived of her chignon on Saturday by its getting entangled with a rope that fell down. You see by this that some of our scenes on board are second to none in "Punch" or "Judy".

Lat 39.27S Long 130.18E Total run 194 miles

73rd day. Tuesday 29th June

We are now commencing to pack and making <u>ready for landing</u>. All over our ship has been painted white, and everything looks so fresh and clean. Today was very bright and the very moon right ahead of us tonight seems to indicate that we are not far from land. There has been sweepstakes going to see what day we make land, tickets 3/- each. Our Head Steward holds the stakes.

Lat 39.31S Long 134.8E Total run 164 miles

74th day. Wednesday 30th June

I shall certainly have very few days more Diaryzing to do. Today the wind is very strong and off the land too (although not yet sighted) so that we are close hauled on the wind making direct for Melbourne with 12 inches of our Deck ploughing the water. We have been going all last night and today at an alarming pace. If the wind does not veer round more against us we shall make Port Philip with this course. We hope the wind won't blow out off the land when we reach Cape Otway (which we fully expect to see tomorrow morning) as this would cause us much tacking about. I along with some others was knocked down on the Poop today by a sea that washed over our ship.

The saloon rung with merriment tonight – everyone so delighted that we are so very near sighting land.

Lat 39.38S Long 139.16E Total run 237 miles

Thursday 1st July 1869

<u>Land, Land Ho!!!</u> And I need not tell you that I am filled with gratitude to God for that blessed sound. Can you judge my feelings now? 13,500 miles away from home. I cannot speak for my fellow passengers, but I know that my heart feels most thankful while gazing at that glorious sight – It is Cape Otway which was first seen at 5 this morning – I write this at 7 tonight, and before us we see the Light houses of the Port Philip Heads (one on each side). We were signalled from the shore at Cape Otway this morning and our arrival has been telegraphed on to Melbourne already – I don't think the Captain will risk going through the Heads tonight.

12 o'clock midnight

Captain has just given orders to lay in till breakfast and keep the Lights of the Heads in view. We have just finished a jolly night's amusement, Mr McKellar and I ordered 3 bottles of champagne to treat the ladies and no less than other 4 were polished off. The Captain and all the Company was present. Numerous toasts were given, also songs etc etc. Mr Sanderson proposed the health of Captain Watson who replied in very suitable terms indeed. The Queen was given by Mr Bourne and the Revd. Mr Grant gave the ladies coupled with the name of the bonnie *Macduff*.

 I must now go to Bed for an hour or two.

[No entry]

Friday 2nd July 1869

Pilot came on board this morning at 3 o'clock and he told us (to the Captain's great satisfaction) that our passage 73 days from land to land was the quickest of this season's ships. The land looks lovely and we are now a good way in Port Philip Bay. There are some very handsome Houses among the trees ashore. The breeze is very faint and we are only going 2 knots an hour. I got the "Argus" from the Pilot, which I am now reading.

 We are all in "full swing" to step ashore on "terra firma". It is now past 3 p.m. and we have about 20 miles to go to the Landing Wharf.

10 pm (1 mile off the Wharf)

Our anchor has just been slipped but it is too late to get ashore any more tonight. Already there are ever so many Custom House officers etc on board examining and sealing up our hatches. I shall have this night yet on board, and if all is well tomorrow morning after breakfast, we shall all go ashore in Boats, so I shall end in wishing one and all of you goodnight and take farewell of my Diary across the Ocean in the good and swift Clipper ship *Macduff*.

– Success to the *Macduff* –

(Signed) Your Alexander Macneill.

Cape Otway Lighthouse, January 1901. The oldest surviving lighthouse in mainland Australia, the light has been in continuous operation since 1848. Perched on the towering sea cliffs at the junction of the Bass Strait and the Southern Ocean, Cape Otway was the first sight of land for thousands of immigrants after months at sea. (State Library of Victoria)

Albatross and Cape pigeons. (Mary Paton)

Sailing ships and steamship in Port Melbourne Docks, 1890. (Photograph by Charles Rudd, State Library of Victoria)

Sailing ships at Woolloomooloo Harbour, Sydney, c 1900.

Port Melbourne around 1870. The ship on the right is the clipper *Superb* built by R & H Green of Blackwall, London, in 1866. A three-masted fully-rigged iron ship, her tonnage was 1451, length 230.3 ft., beam 37.9 ft., depth 23.1 ft. She sailed from Melbourne to London via Cape Horn under her first master, Captain Edward Jones, and the image shows some crew and passengers on board with (top right) a sailor climbing up the rigging. She was broken up in Gibraltar about 1901. (State Library of Victoria)

Collins Street, west of Swanston Street, Melbourne, pictured around 1870. The street was named after David Collins, who later became the first Governor of Tasmania. (State Library of Victoria)

Collins Street, Melbourne, around 1920, with its single-decker trams alongside horse-drawn vehicles.

Melbourne Town Hall under construction around 1869 on the corner of Swanston Street and Collins Street. The foundation stone was laid in 1867 and completed three years later. Advertisements on the hoardings round the building include Clarson Massina's Winter Almanac for 1869; Nightingale's Milliner and Draper's Box; Fry's Caraccas Cocoa; AJ Smith's Book and Stationery Warehouse; Production of Operetta of modern comedy and domestic drama; and Consultation with Dr George Thomas for skin, nervous, and contagious diseases. (State Library of Victoria)

Swanston Street around 1910, showing the Town Hall on the left.

Bridge Road in the borough of Richmond, near Highett Street where Alick stayed in Melbourne. (Richmond Historical Society)

An early image of Swanston Street from Lonsdale Street, Melbourne, in 1870 showing a line-up of horse-drawn buggies. (State Library of Victoria)

St Paul's Cathedral on the corner of Swanston Street and Flinders Street, Melbourne, under construction in the late 1880s. Designed by British architect William Butterfield, it was consecrated in 1891. Hoarding advertisements include Australian Natives Building Society; George and George's Unrivalled Grand Christmas Bazaar; Little's Soluble Phenyle Disinfectant; Sheep Dip; Burke's finest Scotch whisky; and Younger's India Ale. (State Library of Victoria)

St Paul's pictured around 1905. The cathedral's spires were added in the 1920s.

Penultimate page of Alick's journal, transcribed on page 52.

Ferryman Archibald Macneill's gravestone in Kilchattan cemetery, Gigha, with the names of his son Alick and his daughter Margaret added. (James Adam)

Passenger List

Passenger list of the *Macduff*, July 1869, taken from the Unassisted Inward Passenger Lists to Victoria, Public Record Office Victoria. Most of the emigrants were in their thirties, some with young children. Those who travelled cabin class were given a title to their names, while the steerage passengers were noted with only the surname and first name. An additional record from Lloyd's states that there were 44 passengers, including six children, and that six of the adults were Scottish. There are a few minor discrepancies, with Dr Mason entered twice as both William and Alfred, Miss Sullivan listed as both Mary and May, and Alick's age given as 23.

Family name	First name	Age	Family name	First name	Age
Aitkins	Samuel	25	Mason	Emily Miss	5
Bourne	Ralph Mr	24	Mason	William Dr	40
Cameron	Mary Mrs	40	McKellar	James Mr	13
Cleive	Richard S	31	McKellar	Jane Miss	16
Durbridge	Emily	8	McKellar	John Mr	18
Durbridge	George	34	McNamara	Johanna	20
Durbridge	Mary Ann	36	McNamara	Mary	22
Grant	Alfd Wm Revd.	27	McNeill	Alexander Mr	23
Grant	Caroline Mrs	23	O'Connell	Mary	36
Grant	Ernest Alfred	3	Pitou	Leontina	22
Grant	John Perkins	1	Roberts	Henrietta Miss	29
Grieve	Helen Mrs	32	Roberts	Sarah Miss	27
Grieve	John	4	Robson	Wm	28
Grieve	Nelly Miss	1	Sanderson	Thomas Mr	40
Grieve	Robert Mr	39	Shea	Kate	27
Hammond	Sarah	23	Sullivan	Mary	33
Holms	Annie	32	Sullivan	May	33
Holms	John	36	Tait	Ralph	25
Jackson	Joseph William Mr	26	Tasker	Thomas	26
Lacey	Aaron	26	Taylor	Mary	16
Lark	John Vincent	30	Turner	Charles	51
Lee	Charles	34	Watson	Thos T Capt	[no age given]
Mason	Alexander Dr	40	Wheatman	George Edward	23

Log of the *Macduff*, 18 April to 1 July 1869

1	Sunday 18 April	no entry		
2	Monday 19 April	49.27 N	5.21 W	106 miles
3	Tuesday 20 April	48.21 N	6.13 W	147 miles
4	Wednesday 21 April	45.53 N	5.48 W	138 miles
5	Thursday 22 April	45.13 N	7.47 W	105 miles
6	Friday 23 April	44.19 N	8.47 W	77 miles
7	Saturday 24 April	44.28 N	11.10 W	191 miles
8	Sunday 25 April	39.28 N	13.54 W	159 miles
9	Monday 26 April	37.20 N	14.11 W	177 miles
10	Tuesday 27 April	34.49 N	15.23 W	168 miles
11	Wednesday 28 April	32.49 N	17.14 W	125 miles
12	Thursday 29 April	31.10 N	19.30 W	136 miles
13	Friday 30 April	28.23 N	22.38 W	176 miles
14	Saturday 1 May	25.12 N	22.4 W	214 miles
15	Sunday 2 May	22.37 N	23.12 W	167 miles
16	Monday 3 May	20.38 N	23.58 W	127 miles
17	Tuesday 4 May	19.20 N	24.28 W	74 miles
18	Wednesday 5 May	18.17 N	24.50 W	71 miles
19	Thursday 6 May	15.52 N	25.33 W	143 miles
20	Friday 7 May	13.18 N	26.17 W	157 miles
21	Saturday 8 May	10.4 N	26.46 W	174 miles
22	Sunday 9 May	8.24 N	27.0 W	125 miles
23	Monday 10 May	6.7 N	27.0 W	128 miles
24	Tuesday 11 May	3.58 N	26.47 W	129 miles
25	Wednesday 12 May	2.56 N	26.35 W	53 miles
26	Thursday 13 May	1.03 N	26.28 W	113 miles
27	Friday 14 May	0.14 S	26.17 W	76 miles
28	Saturday 15 May	no entry		
29	Sunday 16 May	2.31 S	27.57 W	130 miles
30	Monday 17 May	5.22 S	28.36 W	167 miles
31	Tuesday 18 May	8.19 S	29.11 W	178 miles
32	Wednesday 19 May	12.51 S	29.11 W	217 miles
33	Thursday 20 May	15.30 S	30.38 W	230 miles
34	Friday 21 May	19.30 S	31.13 W	23 miles
35	Saturday 22 May	23.10 S	31.13 W	213 miles
36	Sunday 23 May	25.42 S	29.45 W	174 miles
37	Monday 24 May	26.24 S	27.15 W	53 miles
38	Tuesday 25 May	27.26 S	28.54 W	63 miles

39	Wednesday 26 May	29.37 S	26.59 W	170 miles
40	Thursday 27 May	32.56 S	23.49 W	258 miles
41	Friday 28 May	34.20 S	20.57 W	212 miles
42	Saturday 29 May	34.43 S	19.24 W	82 miles
43	Sunday 30 May	37.6 S	17.40 W	164 miles
44	Monday 31 May	39.5 S	14.22 W	200 miles
45	Tuesday 1 June	40.57 S	11.8 W	185 miles
46	Wednesday 2 June	41.35 S	5.12 W	271 miles
47	Thursday 3 June	42.0 S	1.31 W	70 miles
48	Friday 4 June	42.38 S	4.25 E	248 miles
49	Saturday 5 June	42.34 S	7.31 E	136 miles
50	Sunday 6 June	42.11 S	12.57 E	238 miles
51	Monday 7 June	42.25 S	18.19 E	233 miles
52	Tuesday 8 June	42.15 S	24.5 E	264 miles
53	Wednesday 9 June	42.15 S	27.3 E	132 miles
54	Thursday 10 June	42.16 S	29.59 E	131 miles
55	Friday 11 June	43.37 S	32.47 E	170 miles
56	Saturday 12 June	42.40 S	38.9 E	236 miles
57	Sunday 13 June	42.34 S	43.47 E	246 miles
58	Monday 14 June	42.31 S	50.19 E	286 miles
59	Tuesday 15 June	42.52 S	56.8 E	263 miles
60	Wednesday 16 June	42.8 S	61.48 E	248 miles
61	Thursday 17 June	42.2 S	66.41 E	222 miles
62	Friday 18 June	44.51 S	72.17 E	230 miles
63	Saturday 19 June	42.2 S	77.30 E	292 miles
64	Sunday 20 June	42.16 S	84.1 E	230 miles
65	Monday 21 June	42.1 S	90.45 E	300 miles
66	Tuesday 22 June	44.41 S	97.31 E	302 miles
67	Wednesday 23 June	44.4 S	103.43 E	284 miles
68	Thursday 24 June	41.8 S	109.19 E	254 miles
69	Friday 25 June	40.57 S	115.3 E	292 miles
70	Saturday 26 June	40.16 S	121.53 E	280 miles
71	Sunday 27 June	39.44 S	126.50 E	230 miles
72	Monday 28 June	39.27 S	130.18 E	194 miles
73	Tuesday 29 June	39.31 S	134.8 E	164 miles
74	Wednesday 30 June	39.38 S	139.16 E	237 miles
75	Thursday 1 July	no entry		

Cargo of *Macduff* published in Melbourne *Argus* 4 July 1869

Macduff, from London. - 750 boxes candles, 120 kegs nails, 9 cases locks, 1 case (a picture), 4 cases twine, 4 casks, 31 quarter-casks, cases, Bright Brothers & Co.; 29 packages furniture, 1 case hair seating, W.H. Rocke and Co; 83 packages furniture, S. Solomon and Co.; 1 case gun caps, 8 cases hardware, 50 kegs nails, 4 casks bolts and nuts, Mitchell and Bonneau; 7 packages reaping machine materials, Hutchison and Walker; 100 boxes sheet glass, Swallow and Ariel; 40 cases confections, Lyell and Brown; 5 cases cigars, F.W. Heinicke and Co.; 5 pipes lemon juice, 25 casks pearl barley, 25 casks split peas, 10 cases patent groats, 100 cases black currant fruits, 30 cases (pints) salad oil, 10 cases (half-pints) castor oil, 12 casks currants, 6 cases Epsom salts, 20 cases lemon peel, 25 cases kippered herrings, McEwan and Co.; 65 barrels crushed sugar, 255 cases cocoa, 50 cases baking powder, 10 cases jelly, 5 cases paste, 45 cases mustard, 50 cases starch, 77 cases salmon, 1 case, Connell, Watson and Hogarth; 1898 bars iron, 40 cases galvanised iron, 5 bundles steel, 425 bundles hoops, 40 iron wheels, 4 stoves, 228 arms and boxes, 3 casks 48 kegs nails, 13 anvils, 69 casks scythe stones, 5 casks hardware, 3 crates tubs, 8 boilers, 2 cases, 3 bundles, 2 packages (a pump), 11 cases vestas, 25 iron kegs, 84 casks, 214 kegs, 61 cases, Jas. McEwan and Co.; 100 cases, Lyall and Co.; 33 hhds.,102 quarter-casks, White Brothers and Co.; 15 hhds, 70 quarter-casks rum, 50 hhds, 100 quarter-casks Fanning and Co.; 240 bundles wire, McCallum and Co.; 720 deals, Wilshin and Leighton; 4 tanks, 5 bales, James Henty and Co.; 12 cases raisins, 675 deals, 20 bales, Turnbull and Co.; 6 axles, 9 cases, Box and Son; 86 casks, Fitch and French; 6 bales, W. Detmold; 62 pockets hops, 100 boxes tin, 45 hhds., 84 barrels, 260 kegs, 20 cases, Geo. Martin and Co.; 8 bundles tubs, 8 puncheons, 3 casks, 1 hhd., 60 kegs, 2 crates, 25 bundles, 14 cases, Thos. Raine; 12 barrow wheels, 36 casks, 15 kegs, 5 cases, Brooks and Co.; 106 kegs nails, E. Baines; 10 cases, Wilkie, Webster & Co.; 24 cases, J. Kronheimer and Co.; 1 cask meal, 8 crates bottles, B.S. Dawson; 86 kegs nails, 14 cases galvanised iron, 20 ingots tin, J. Ellis and Co.; 20 barrels currants, 128 cases raisins, 52 packages, H.W. Farrar and Co.; 77 trunks,1 case, Buttner and Co.; 1 case, W.C. Clifton; 14 cases, J.Dynon; 57 cases, Lange and Thoneman; 81 boxes type, Gordon and Gotch; 4 cases, W.G. Mayfield; 4 bales, W. and N.G. Elder; 105 quarter-casks, Curcier and Adet; 4 cases books, Gimblett and Co.; 2 cases pictures, R. Black; 2 cases, J. Volum; 26 cases galvanised iron, Croaker, Scott and Co.; 3 cases, 1 cask, 1 bale, R. Hodgson; 2 cases books, Public Library; 30 cases chairs, Wallach Bros.; 7 cases, 1 bale, Kerrand Young; 1,000 boxes candles, Joshua Bros.; 4 cases, J.C. Evans; 1 case, Alexander Macfarlan and Co.; 147 trunks, 20 bales, 86 cases, L. Stevenson and Sons; 68 bundles baskets, 12 rollers, 6 nests, 20 rolls, 6 casks, 2 hhds., 23 cases, Whitney, Chambers and Co.; 1 case, R.S. Neave and Co.; 8 cases, King and Parsons; 15 cases, W. Martin and Co.; 6 cases, Brasch Bros. and Salenger; 50 cases, 11 bales, Robertson and Moffat; 40 bags glue, Wilson and Co.; 500 boxes candles, 2 cases oil of lemon, 10 kegs, 12 cases, Moore and Co.; 15 cases, Gill and Thorpe; 9 cases, Banks, bros., Bell and Co.; 220 boxes, 140 casks, 25 bundles, 200 cases, W. Peterson and Co.; 100 boxes candles, 130 cases, 50 boxes, 15 casks, D. Masterton and Co.; 20 barrels, 139 cases, G. and G. Shaw; 8 casks, 16 cases, P. Falk and Co.; 6 cases boots, J. Bloomington; 3 bales, 3 cases, Cramond and Co.; 20 cases, Wiseman Brothers; 6 bales, 92 cases, 1 cask, Geo. Robertson; 1 case, Lazarus Brothers; 4 trunks, 27 cases, G. Gibson; 6 trunks, 3 cases, Sargood, Son, and Co.; 5 bales, 157 cases, Paterson, Ray, Palmer, and Co.; 11 cases, P. McBride; 139 bundles, 3 casks, 8 cases, 2 crates, J. and S. Danks; 1 piano, J. Fairchild; 2 cases, W. Dawson; 25,000 slates, 20 rolls lead, 8 cases galvanised iron, 1 pipe, Thomas Warburton; 4 cases sheet iron, Hughes and Harvey; 120 drums oil, 12 casks, 1 bale, H. Jackson; 40 boxes tin, Freeman and Co.; 1 bin (2,400 bushels) malt, 99 cases brandy, 6 butts 18 quarter-casks wine, 50 hhd. beer, 20 casks oil, 2 case acids, 6 cases hosiery, 9 cases furniture, 30 bags cocoa, 22 bales paper, 6 tierces red lead, 25 casks nails, 4 casks lasts, 2 bales leather, 6 pieces (printing machine), 3 cases wool, 47 tons firebricks, 40 tanks, 24 pockets, 60 quarter-casks, 1,000 boxes, 114 cases and packages.

Acknowledgements

The author would like to express thanks and appreciation to the following for their generous help in the research of this book:

UK: Aberdeen Art Gallery and Museums; James Adam; Kenneth Allan; Argyll and Bute Council Archives; Maureen Bell; Dr Moira Burgess; John Edwards, Keeper of Science and Maritime History, and Meredith Greiling, Assistant Keeper of Maritime History, Aberdeen Maritime Museum; Eleanor Harris, Local Studies Librarian, Argyll and Bute Library Service; Isle of Gigha Heritage Trust; Valerie Gillies; Margaret Johnson; Alasdair McNeill; Angus Martin; Ewan McNeill; Mhairi McNeill; Mitchell Library, Glasgow; National Archives of Scotland; Jim Swan.

Australia: Bill Bourke, Curator, Sydney Heritage Fleet; Paul Dee and Imaging Department, State Library of Victoria; Craig Mackenzie and Sarah Schmitt, National Library of Australia; Kevin McNamara; Sue McNamara; Dr Kim McNamara; Dr Donald McNeill; Mary and Ian Paton; Richmond and Burnley Historical Society; Royal Historical Society of Victoria.

And to all my friends for their encouragement and patience in listening to endless monologues about emigration and 19th century clippers.

INDEX

Aberdeen, 3-4, 11, 13, 30-1, 33-4, 36, 66
Achnaha, 1, 6, 8
Alarm, 26
albatross, 16, 43-4, 46
amusements, 21
Ardminish, 5, 7-8, back cover
Argo, 25
Ariel, 13
Aska, 8
Australia, 1-3, 13, 15, 19-20, 22-3, 29, 36, 47, 49-51, 53, 59, 66
berth, 3-4, 19, 25, 39
cabin, 3-4, 15, 17, 19-20, 26-8, 38, 49, 61
Cabot, 23
Canary Islands, 24
canvas, 2, 14, 40-1, 43, 47, 49
Cape of Good Hope, 14, 39-40, 43-4, 46
Cape de Verde, 27
Cape Otway, 18, 49-53
Cape pigeon, 43, 53
Captain Watson, 4, 13-23, 25-8, 37-45, 49, 51- 2
cargo, 13, 30, 50, 64
China tea race, 2, 13, 32
clipper, 1-2, 4, 11, 13, 18, 30-3, 55, 66
crew, 16-7, 39, 55
Customs House officers, 13, 52
Cutty Sark, 13, 32
diary, 1, 4, 18, 20-1, 23
doctor, 15, 17, 23, 28
emigration, 2-3, 66
equator, crossing, 2, 16
ferry, 5-8
ferryman, 1, 5, 14
figurehead, 4, 11
food, 15
Furnace Abbey, 23
gale(s), 14-15, 40, 42-7, 49
Gigha, 1-2, 5-8, 10, 16, 18, 20, 25, 60, 66, back cover

Glasgow, 2-4, 10, 16, 25, 46, 66
gold, 2, 13
Great Britain, 20
Greenwich, 13, 32, 45, 48-9
ice, 23, 43
Ida Arbacht, 37
Jho Sho Maru, 33
journal, 2, 4, 10, 12, 18, 35, 60
Kintyre, 1-2, 5, 7, 9, 20
knots, 14-5, 19-21, 23, 27, 41-4, 46-7, 49, 51-2
ladies, 3-4, 14, 17, 19-21, 23, 27-8, 37, 40, 44-9, 51-2
land, 2-3, 14, 17-8, 20-1, 24, 27, 40, 47, 49-53
livestock, 47
Lloyd's, 4, 14, 40, 61
log, 19, 22, 45, 48, 62
Macduff, 1-2, 4, 11-5, 19, 22, 29, 31, 34, 40-1, 46, 50, 52, 61-2, 64
Madeira, 14, 23-4
Mayoress, 24
meals, 15
Melbourne, 2-4, 11, 13, 18-20, 22, 25, 29, 33-4, 38-40, 42-52, 54-9, 64, back cover
mizzen mast, 4, 16, 28, 42, 50
Oriental, 13
Partick, 2, 10, 25
passengers, 2-3, 5, 14-7, 19, 21, 26-7, 37-8, 40, 43-4, 47, 49-50, 52, 55, 61
pilot, 19, 52
polar star, 37
Port Phillip, 2, 13, 18, 29, 50-2
rigging, 16, 28, 32, 41-2, 55
rum, 13, 16-7, 28, 39, 42, 64
sailors, 15-6, 22, 24, 27-8, 37-42, 44-5, 47, 49-50
sail(s), 2, 4, 7, 14-5, 18, 20-1, 25, 27, 41, 43, 45, 50
Scotland, 1-2, 16, 18, 22, 37, 39, 51, 66

service, 9, 13, 16, 19, 22, 26, 37, 40, 42, 47, 66
sextant, 14, 37, 45
ships, 4, 9, 14-26, 36, 39-41
shipyard, 13, 31, 33, 42, 45, 48, 50, 52, 54
signalise, 4, 14, 22, 24, 40
Southern Cross, 14, 26
squall, 15, 37, 41, 43, 49
Star of Peace, 13
stars, 14, 21, 26-7, 38
steamer, 5, 8, 14, 19-21, 33, 46
steerage, 3, 15, 44, 61
Superb, 55
Taeping, 13
Tasmania, 38, 56
Thermopylae, 13, 32-3
Trade Winds, 14, 25, 27, 39
Tropics, 25, 28, 37, 41
True Briton, 13
water, 2, 4, 6, 13, 15-7, 23-4, 27-8, 37-40, 42-4, 49, 51
weather, 14-5, 20-1, 24, 26-8, 39, 41-7, 49-50
Westmoreland, 2